Ghosts of St. Louis

The Lemp Mansion and Other Eerie Tales

Bryan Alaspa

Schiffer Publishing Ltd®

4880 Lower Valley Road Atglen, Pennsylvania 19310

Published by Schiffer Publishing Ltd.
4880 Lower Valley Road
Atglen, PA 19310
Phone: (610) 593-1777; Fax: (610) 593-2002
E-mail: Info@schifferbooks.com

For the largest selection of fine reference books on this and related subjects, please visit our web
site at **www.schifferbooks.com**

We are always looking for people to write books on new and related subjects. If you have an idea
for a book please contact us at the above address.

This book may be purchased from the publisher.
Include $3.95 for shipping.
Please try your bookstore first.
You may write for a free catalog.

In Europe, Schiffer books are distributed by
Bushwood Books
6 Marksbury Ave.
Kew Gardens
Surrey TW9 4JF England
Phone: 44 (0) 20 8392-8585; Fax: 44 (0) 20 8392-9876
E-mail: info@bushwoodbooks.co.uk
Website: www.bushwoodbooks.co.uk
Free postage in the U.K., Europe; air mail at cost.

Author Photo by Scott Prince, copyright 2006.
Copyright © 2007 by Bryan W. Alaspa

Library of Congress Control Number: 2007927369

Designed by Mark David Bowyer
Type set in Grasshopper / New Baskerville BT

ISBN: 978-0-7643-2688-2
Printed in China

Contents

Foreword:
A Haunted City

The city of St. Louis is a modern metropolis. It is best known as the place where the Gateway Arch resides overlooking the Mississippi River. It is the place where the St. Louis Cardinals play baseball. It is a city known and associated with Lewis and Clark.

Yes, it is a modern city with all of the modern conveniences of any modern city. However, St. Louis is also an old city. It is a city with old buildings. It is a city with legends. It is a city that once had some of the wealthiest people in the country in residence. It is even a city that brought beer to the nation.

But it is also a city that has a few characteristics that are unique to other cities. For example, much of the land in and around what is now St. Louis was Native American land. Just across the river, in Illinois, are the Cahokia Mounds, a kind of relic of Native American culture. There are Indian burial grounds all around.

St. Louis, and, indeed, much of Missouri, is nestled on a solid foundation of limestone. This means that much of downtown St. Louis is actually a network of caves and limestone tunnels. One of the reputed properties of limestone is that it can withhold energy, such as life energy and essence. At times, it is believed, the limestone will release that energy, and events from long ago will play out again. People, at these times, will be seen walking down the street and then suddenly vanish.

St. Louis is actually one of the most-haunted cities, not just in this country, but in the entire world. More reports of ghosts and hauntings come from this part of the country than even some of the oldest cities in the world. It is a haunted city. It is an American city. It is a city filled with ghosts.

Part One:
An American Story

The city of St. Louis, in 1838, was truly a frontier town. The entire town was booming. New people from all around the world were streaming into the city by the bend in the Mississippi River. They brought with them all of their traditions and beliefs and talents from wherever they came. St. Louis was soon to become a city that introduced wondrous and amazing new things to the entire country.

St. Louis started down the road to becoming a huge city in the United States in 1817, when a steamboat by the name of the *Zebulon M. Pike* arrived. It was the start of the steamboat era and the use of the Mississippi as a major thoroughfare and route of transporting people and goods in this country. Rapids, located just north of St. Louis, meant that the city was as far north as you could safely travel on the Mississippi River. St. Louis became a boomtown as it turned into the largest port city west of New York, and then the most populous city west of Pittsburgh.

Once the city had become as big and prosperous as it appeared, by the 1830s and 1840s, a great influx of immigrants began to settle in the area. Germany, Bohemia, Italy, and Ireland caused the population of St. Louis to explode. The city had a population of about 20,000 people in 1840, and by 1860, there were 160,000 people living next to the Mississippi.

The Louisiana Purchase was not that far into the past, when a man named Johann Adam Lemp decided that St. Louis was the place where he would settle. He had modest dreams like most immigrants.

He wanted to be successful. He wanted to set up a store. He wanted to sell to the people who were streaming into this town as it exploded into a city. But he never believed he would revolutionize the way people would celebrate—or get drunk! Johann just believed people might like to drink a beer or two when they visited his store.

There are a lot of people who can probably tell the stories of all of the major beer manufacturers in this country—each of them involved and detailed. The Anheuser-Busch names are probably the best known of those coming out of St. Louis. Their proud brewery still stands on the south-side of the city, not far from the river. You can take tours there. You can sample the beer. You can stop by the stable and view the famous Clydesdales. The same, however, cannot be said for the name of Lemp.

The fact that most beer drinkers probably do not know the name Lemp is testament to the story of this family. Nevertheless, had you been living in St. Louis in the late 1800s, you mostly likely would have known the name. In fact, you would have known all about the family. You would have known about the beautiful Lillian Lemp and her nickname, "The Lavender Lady." You probably would have enjoyed some of Lemp's famous "Falstaff" beer at a local pub. But, considering you probably don't know the name of Lemp, this is very telling.

In many ways, the story of the Lemps, their brewery, their success, their failures, and their mansion are a true American story. This is a country built on immigrants. No one, save the Native Americans, actually came from this country. The entire purpose of America is and was for someone to leave the place where they were born and find success somewhere else. America was, and is, the land of opportunity. Johann Adam Lemp knew that at the time.

What makes it more of an American story was that Johann Lemp achieved success. He achieved so much success, he changed the way the entire country drank and bought beer. In fact, he died a millionaire, most likely confident that his heirs would continue the Lemp name and tradition down throughout history.

In its own way, the Lemp story is American because it turns out so tragic. America has always had a love for tragedy. The Lemp story is a story that has been read and re-read and reviewed many times over. The divorce between Lillian and William Lemp made national news and was a countrywide scandal. In their own way, the tabloid frenzy over scandal was a bit of a Lemp invention as well. They achieved and then they lost, and in between was a story of love and deceit and betrayal and sex and suicide.

To celebrate their success, the Lemps built themselves a mansion. It was a huge thing that easily set them apart from everyone else in St. Louis at the time. It was a monument to the success of alcohol and America's insatiable thirst—probably meant to stand the test of time, and house Lemps into eternity. It has become famous, but probably not for the reasons the Lemps originally intended it to.

The city of St. Louis is very much former American Indian land. The Cahokia Mounds, once a large Indian city, is located just across the Mississippi in Illinois. Other Indian cities and burial grounds dot the landscape in and around St. Louis and throughout central Illinois. Built upon a past going back hundreds of years, St. Louis is filled with spirits and hauntings and is reportedly one of the most haunted cities not only in this country, but the entire world. And despite this history and the sheer number of reported hauntings, few are as notoriously haunted as the Lemp Mansion.

In November of 1980, *Life* magazine declared the Lemp Mansion one of the most haunted places in America. Again, in a truly American story, this declaration only succeeded in bringing mystique, glamour, and success back to a place that had so long stood for tragedy and death and failure. The Lemp Mansion still stands. You can eat a meal there. You can take a tour. You can see a dinner play. You can spend the night there. People go hoping to see something they cannot explain, and it seems that they are seldom disappointed.

Even without the hauntings, the story of the Lemp family and the empire they created and then lost is a powerful tale. It is a soap opera in the truest American sense. It is a story of a family who attained almost unimaginable wealth, but of people who were victims of their times. In a day and age when mental health was not something seriously considered, and depression something someone could just get over if they tried hard enough, they were doomed. These days, the Lemp family could have been diagnosed and treated and perhaps medicated for the mental illnesses that appeared to have run rampant through their lives. In the late 1800s and early 1900s, they had no hope. Tragedy was their destiny.

To understand the phenomenon of the Lemp Mansion and the spirits that are purported to still live there, you need to understand the family that built the house. You need to know the tale of a family that reached the highest of heights, only to fall apart at their own hands. It's a truly American tale of success and failure. Along the way, there is plenty of drama and madness and sex and betrayal. To understand the hauntings of the Lemp Mansion, you need to get to know the Lemps themselves and the empire they built.

Chapter One:
The Common History

Initially, I had hoped to keep myself out of the telling of the story of the Lemp family and the mansion that bears their name. However, as I began to research this remarkable story, it became more and more evident that I would have to insert myself into the tale. I was going to have to visit the mansion myself. More importantly, I was going to have to try and spend the night there.

I met a remarkable woman on the night that I spent sleeping in William Lemp, Sr.'s bedroom. Her name was Betsy, and she is a woman who claims to be able to detect, speak to, and guide spirit energies and spirits. I am not here to claim that she either *does* or *does not* have that ability. I can only testify to the fact that she has a great sense of humor, a deep interest in the mansion and the tales surrounding it, and a kind of love for the legacy and life of the Lemps.

I will have more to tell you about my eventful night at the Lemp Mansion. There were some amazing things to see and hear. However, the time I spent talking to Betsy was some of the most interesting. You see, Betsy has spent nearly a decade working in the Lemp Mansion. She gives tours of the place. She talks to the ghosts and spirits there. She gets their stories.

What came out of my talk with Betsy was that there are two stories of the Lemps. There is what I have come to refer to as the "Common History." This is the history you are likely to find if you go online and do a search for the Lemp mansion. This is the history I want to present first—a tale presented as cold, hard facts and most commonly believed and accepted.

What I learned is that there is another history. This is the history that Betsy, and people who are like her, claim to get directly from the ghosts themselves. The tales diverge severely in a number of places.

So, let's take a look at the history of the Lemp Mansion and how a family changed the way the United States and the Midwest, in particular, took a drink after work.

Chapter Two: Coming to America

The town of Eschwege, Germany looks very much like you'd picture most towns looking when you think of small German towns. It has those traditional German-looking buildings like you see in movies set in Germany, with green lands and a river running through the town. Eschwege is in the state known as Hesse and is the capital of the Werra-Meissner-Kreis district sitting directly on the river Werra. The district is located in the extreme northeastern part of Germany. Eschwege is the kind of town most people would probably see on a tour of Germany and not think twice about it. Its most famous attraction is a four-day drinking and music festival known as the Johannisfest.

Johann Adam Lemp was born in Eschwege. Not much is known about his life before he came to St. Louis in 1838. Essentially, he exchanged one river town for another. Given the timing of his arrival there, he was most likely just another immigrant face in a town bustling with immigrant and steamboat traffic—another man with an accent who was looking to start his own business. The one thing that Johann Adam Lemp did have, that the other immigrants did not have, however, was a recipe for beer that had been passed down through his family for generations.

Johann did not set out to completely change what America was drinking, though. No, his original intent was to open a dry good store, and that is exactly what he did when he first came to St. Louis. Johann set up his small grocery store at the corners of Delmar and 6th Streets. He sold groceries and common household items, including vinegar he brewed himself. The key factor that would change his life, however, was the homemade beer he also sold from his store. Johann brewed the beer himself from a recipe his father had taught him. It was a kind of beer that America was not very familiar with at that time.

Most beer sold and consumed in the United States at that time was of the dark-ale variety. English beers were the most common. These beers were as dark as tar, heavy, bold, and strongly flavored. Johann had a beer he called a "lager" and it was golden in color, light-tasting, and very different from the ales that everyone else was selling. Johann soon found he didn't have quite the space or the facilities to brew enough lager beer to meet the demand.

By 1840, the demand was so high that Johann was able to sell off the grocery store and buy land to build a brewery. He bought land right near where the Gateway Arch now stands and began brewing his golden lager beer to the city along with his vinegar. He built a pub attached directly to the brewery, and sold the beer that way at first. He soon found that even that was not enough room to meet the demand and the crowds of people clamoring for the new beer.

Johann needed to expand and, after some quick searching, discovered St. Louis had something that was just perfect for brewing lager beer and brewing it in large quantities: limestone caves. By 1845, however, the beer was selling so well that Johann finally gave up the brewing and selling of vinegar and began to focus strictly on alcohol.

The main ingredient that gives beer its taste is the use of yeast in the brewing process. The yeast used in most of the ales that were around then, and now, are allowed to do their work at higher temperatures. This creates a fruitier taste that is common to most ales. The key to a lager is reducing the activity of the yeast. Since yeast is actually a living organism, the way to reduce the activity of the yeast as it works is to reduce the temperature at which it ferments, and then storing the lager for longer periods of time.

The problem then is that you have to keep the yeast and the brew cold for that longer period of time without the yeast dying and turning the beer into a horrific-smelling, undrinkable swill. If you do it right, however, you get the crisp yellow-colored liquid that most people associate with modern American beers.

So, as you can see, the most important key to successfully brewing lager beer is to keep the liquid cold. This was not an easy thing to do in an age where refrigeration was largely a theory and not something very much in practice. And this was the primary reason the darker English ales were so popular before Johann began brewing. Johann discovered, though, that St. Louis was built on a large network of limestone caves. (In fact, much of Missouri is built on limestone, and one of the things limestone does well is keep things cool.)

Missouri is a network of limestone caves that stretches nearly from border to border. In the Ozark Mountains, there is a network of caves known as the Meramec Caverns. If you drive down to St. Louis and through Missouri, you can see signs promoting tours of those caverns. It was the place where Jesse James and his gang would hide out during their key robbing years. One of the most interesting things about the advertising about the Meramec Caverns is that they promote themselves as being a cool sixty degrees year around.

While the Ozark mountains have some of the best-known caverns in the state, the city of St. Louis is also located over a rather infamous network of caves. Most of downtown St. Louis, to this day, is located over such a network. Businesses, over the years, have used these caves to create underground walkways. The Native Americans knew about the caves and used them for hideouts. There are stories of haunted caves below St. Louis that supposedly contain the spirits of a Native American couple who starved to death there.

These caves were perfect for Johann and his brewing needs. While keeping his brew cool when he was making smaller batches in his pub was relatively easy, producing the massive quantities that the public was clamoring for would prove difficult. He found his solution underground and with the large body of water that runs right past St. Louis and had turned a small town into the bustling boomtown it had become.

Just south of the city limits of St. Louis and at the modern-day corner of Cherokee and De Menil Place, Johann found a large limestone cave that also had easy access to the Mississippi River. The caves were, of course, cool to begin with and very large. He could easily fit the large containers he'd planned on using to produce massive amounts of his beer. He also discovered that when ice formed on the Mississippi River, he could bring huge chunks of it into the caves and they would stay, not just cool, but cold. The ideal temperature for brewing lager beer is between forty-four to fifty-five degrees Fahrenheit. With the chunks of ice in place in the already cool temperatures, there was now the perfect atmosphere to brew lager beer in large quantities.

With his caves in place and packed with ice, Johann Adam Lemp founded Lemp's Western Brewing Company. He began to make beer that satisfied the craving in St. Louis. In 1858, the beer he created won a first-place prize for beer at the annual St. Louis Fair. Things were looking up for the Lemp family and the family became one of the richest and most prominent in St. Louis. Johann Lemp was a millionaire by 1862.

While Johann Adam Lemp was creating his brewing empire, he was also creating a family. Little is know about his wife, but it is known that he had at least one son. He named his son William, and it would be William he would pass along his fortune and his brewing company to when he died.

Johann Adam Lemp passed away in 1862. No national record is found about his death in newspapers from the time. There was nothing particularly spectacular about his death. He died quietly.

More than likely, he was sure that his legacy was secured. His family and his company were one of the most prominent in the brewing industry, not only in St. Louis, but around the country. He had managed to make millions even in the 1800s, which would have to translate to billions in today's dollars. His son had expressed interest in expanding the family business upon taking it over. Probably, Johann Lemp would have said he was certain his family's name would go down in history as revolutionizing beer and beer-making, along with names like Pabst, Anheuser-Bush, and Coors.

In many ways, Johann Lemp was correct. His family would indeed become famous. In some ways, his family would become *infamous*. As the most prominent family in St. Louis, he almost certainly did not realize how much his family would be followed and scrutinized by the press and media of the time. What he could not possibly know is that his family's name would become well-known, but only in association with words like suicide, divorce, betrayal—and ghosts.

Chapter Three:
The Founder's Son

William Lemp appears in photographs of the time as a man with a kind of twinkle in his eyes and the slightest hint of a smile on his lips. He has a good head of gray and black hair, and a bush beard and mustache that was common among men at the time. He also appears to have been a man with dreams of increasing the Lemp fortunes, and doing so rapidly, as judged by his near-immediate activities upon inheriting the family fortune and business.

William saw the demand for his father's beer on the increase and felt that the facilities used to make that beer should increase as well. William bought a five-block area around the storage facility on Cherokee and began a major renovation and expansion of the brewery. By 1864, two years after he took over, a new plant was standing at Cherokee and Carondolet Avenue. Before long, the increasing demand made it necessary for the Lemp Brewery to use the entire five blocks for making their beer.

The Lemp name became famous with the creation of their "Falstaff" beer. The name exists to this day, but no longer has a relation to the Lemps. The name was sold along with much of the family's beer-making abilities after the turn of the century coinciding with a turn in their family fortunes. However, by the time William took over the business, the Falstaff name was famous. By the 1890s, Falstaff set another milestone in beer consumption in this country by becoming the first lager beer distributed across the entire country. The Lemps were also the first brewery to create a coast-to-coast distribution method for its beer.

In short, under William Lemp, the Lemp name began to symbolize wealth and power in St. Louis and had a firm grip on the entire beer-making industry in that city. In addition, the Lemp name was becoming famous across the country. It seemed like the family name was destined to be illustrious forever. Their fortunes continued to grow. They were employers of hundreds of St. Louis workers, and their plant and distribution centers were under constant expansion, updating, and renovations.

William met and fell in love with a woman named Julia Feickert. They were soon married. It was this relationship that would create a major and key piece of the Lemp legend. Julia's father, Jacob, built a house. Rumor has it that William financed the building and then bought it outright from Jacob once it was finished.

The mansion was impressive, to say the least, even by modern standards. Because it was a short distance from the brewery, some rooms within the mansion served as brewery offices. The house was also a short distance from the Mississippi at the corner of Cherokee and De Menil Place just south of what is now downtown St. Louis.

The entire brewery and mansion were imposing and great feats of architecture. The newly remodeled brewery was designed in an Italian Renaissance style and was full of brick cornices and arched windows. The mansion was remarkable when William purchased it. But he seemed to have a knack for never being entirely satisfied with property upon owning it, because he almost immediately began expanding and renovating the house.

William discovered that the terrain underneath the mansion had great potential as well. The same caves that were being used by the brewery, also wound their way under the streets and under the mansion. In fact, by using diggers to dig out a walkway into a portion of the caves used for lagering, William discovered that he could walk from the mansion to the brewery without having to walk above ground at all.

Technology began to advance when it came to keeping things cool as the nineteenth century came to a close. Refrigeration became more common and the caves beneath the brewery were not needed any longer for brewing beer. This did not pose a problem for William, however. His desire to build and improve the mansion seemed to extend below ground, and he began to remodel the earth as well.

A large chamber that had been carved out of the limestone was converted into a theater. A stage was created and crude scenery was made. There were stone seats in the form of large stone benches shaped in true theater fashion. There were even primitive floodlights used to illuminate the stage. The Lemps, being the richest family in town it is rumored—and quite possibly likely—hired the most prominent actors from the vaudeville circuits to perform for them down beneath the streets. The theater even had a spiral staircase carved out of stone that lead right onto Cherokee street.

The old Lemp Factory and Brewery.

Just a few feet away from the theater, the Lemps created another underground luxury. A large limestone reservoir was dug and filled with water that was originally used for lagering. William changed that once the underground lagering was put by the wayside, and turned the limestone pit into a lined swimming pool. The key to enjoying the pool was that hot water was piped into the pool from the boilers in the brewery for year-round and comfortable swimming, despite the coolness of the caves.

Finally, just a few feet away from both the stage and swimming pool, William also had a ballroom constructed. Like the other rooms, it was massive, impressive, and lavishly decorated. The Lemps were able to have parties and entertain large groups entirely underground.

This network of caves was easily accessible through doorways and hallways located beneath the mansion. As the family fortunes turned and Prohibition turned brewing beer into an illegal activity, these caves were abandoned. Rumor has it that the pool and theater are still there, however, and that the theater may still have some of its crumbling scenery.

The problems with William began with his son. He had two, actually, and they were William, Jr. and Frederick. Without a doubt and, evidently no attempt to hide the fact, it was Frederick who was his father's favorite. Almost from birth, it was Frederick who was groomed by his father to take over the Lemp business. It was Frederick who was taught the business and how to brew the now-famous Lemp beer.

Pictures of Frederick show a handsome gentleman with black hair and a black mustache. He looks, if anything, just a tad too thin, and maybe that was an indication of things to come. What *is* known is that Frederick was a workaholic. He spent all hours of the day and night working at the brewery. He worked and toiled to make himself worthy of the Lemp name and the Lemp fortune. Whether he was driven to work as much as he was *pushed* into work is not entirely clear. What *is* clear is that the long hours took a toll on the young man. The apple of his father's eye, Frederick Lemp may have quite literally worked himself to death and died of heart failure at the age of twenty-eight in 1901. The exact reasons behind the heart failure are also not clear, since autopsies and post-mortems were not nearly as common back then as they are now. He was merely described as feeling ill and passing away from heart failure.

In fact, hope had risen for Frederick for some time which may have increased the tragedy of the situation. Frederick had begun to complain of ill health and he was sent to California to a kind of spa to recover. He was showing signs of improvement when things suddenly took a turn for the worst. He never improved again.

Before Frederick passed away, William Lemp, Sr. also made friends with other brewers in the Midwest. The Lemps helped the Anheuser and Busch families get their brewery up and running in the St. Louis area. William also became very good friends with another Frederick, this being Frederick Pabst. In fact, according to most accounts, Frederick Pabst was William's closest friend and confidant. Whether or not his son, Frederick, happened to be named for his closest friend is not clear, but it is certainly odd that two people named Frederick would bring heartbreak to William Lemp and send him spiraling down the road that others would follow.

William was devastated when his son passed away. According to reports from the time and from co-workers and acquaintances, William became increasingly withdrawn. Whereas before, William saw nothing but success, the need to expand, and a desire to cause his empire, his brewery, and his house to grow, he began to show less and less interest in the business. He began to be seen less and less in public. Considering how public and prominent the family had become in St. Louis society at the time, this was saying something. He began showing up at work by taking only the underground caverns. He still came to the office every day, but he seemed distracted and very nervous. He was not able to focus on work and showed little interest in business endeavors that the Lemp Brewery might want to expand into.

In 1904, what appears to have been the final blow to William's psyche occurred with Frederick Pabst dying very suddenly. What is interesting about Pabst's death is that though he had been suffering from a life-threatening illness, he had been showing signs of improvement. Suddenly, right after the new year, he took a turn for the worst. Pabst had family in St. Louis, and William was notified very quickly.

William lost all desire to work after the death of his friend. His interest managed to decrease. He became jittery, anti-social, distracted, and unsettled. He began to become physically sick. He was seldom, if at all, seen in public. His mental health began to decline, and things finally reached the point where he could take it no longer on February 13, 1904.

William started the morning relatively normally that day, although he slept in later than normal. Given his recent propensity for illness, this probably did not seem too unusual to the servants and people in the house. His wife and his other son, William Jr., had left for the day when the senior William awoke, descended the stairs, and sat down for breakfast.

Nothing seemed amiss during the morning meal. William ate his food and then commented to one of the servants that he was not feeling well again, and that he wanted to go back to bed. He excused himself from the table and ascended the stairs leading to the bedrooms on the second floor of the mansion. At around nine-thirty that morning, he entered his bedroom and found his .38 caliber Smith & Wesson revolver. He lifted the gun to his temple and pulled the trigger.

The mansion was not an empty place. The house was full of servants in the kitchens and taking care of the house. Workers from the brewery even used some of the rooms as offices. Servants ran to second floor at the sound of the shot, and others were sent blocks to the brewery to find William, Jr. William ran home, up the stairs, and kicked in the door to find his father's body, the gun still clutched in his hand.

William Lemp had lead his family further than his father had probably dared dream. The Lemp name was now known across the country, and their fortunes had grown to the point that they were the most prominent citizens in St. Louis. Once again, despite the setback, it seemed like the family fortune had nowhere to go but up. However, under the rule of William Lemp, Jr. the Lemp brewing fortune and family history was about to take a very scandalous turn.

Chapter Four:
The Wild Child

In November of 1904, William Lemp, Jr. took over as president of the William J. Lemp Brewing Company. In many ways, he was what we have come to think of as the spoiled rich kid. He loved expensive things. He had a knack and tendency for partying. He was a notorious womanizer. In the end, he would bring about one of the biggest scandals in St. Louis history.

As far as the family business was concerned, it seems, in the commonly-told history of the mansion, as if Billy had little interest. He built country homes. He hired servants and filled the mansion with them. He bought wardrobes of the most expensive clothing and began buying expensive pieces of art. He had costly and lavish carriages to cart him around as well, much like a rich kid buying himself a sports car today.

Billy, by many accounts, was a very intense man. He also had a very cruel streak. He was known to conduct animal fights in the limestone caverns beneath the mansion. He was also fond of carrying a gun with him. And he not only carried it with him all the time, but he had a tendency to brandish it about whenever the mood seemed to suit him. He would pull the gun on a friend if he saw fit. He would pull the gun on someone who bumped into him on the street. He would pull the gun on someone who he felt looked at him wrong when he was in his carriage. Finally, he would keep the gun under his pillow at night—but with the barrel pointed at his wife.

The one thing that Billy truly seemed to love was women. He married one of the finest in the city in 1899, when he married Lillian Handlan. Lillian was the daughter of a wealthy manufacturer. The marriage was a huge affair, as the two wealthy families united. Their activities together were recorded eagerly by the St. Louis press.

Lillian seemed to enjoy spending the Lemp fortune almost as eagerly as William did. She apparently had a penchant for wearing the color and scent of Lavender. In fact, she wore the color so much, she actually got the nickname, "The Lavender Lady," and had her carriage horses' harnesses dyed the unique color. She spent money on clothing and other extravagances.

Lillian was not a very tall woman. According to account, she was only four-feet-two inches tall. Despite this, she was a strong woman, able to hold her own even against a dominant personality like Billy Lemp. In fact, one of the few original pieces of history still in the Lemp Mansion is a huge fish mounted, and now stationed, above the bar. At one time, that bar was the mansion's library. The fish is enormous and a small plaque underneath it indicates that it was caught by Lillian Lemp on a trip to Florida and then presented to her father-in-law.

The brewing scene, by 1906, had started to change for Billy, and the company he found himself the head of. It was not a change that bode well for the Lemp fortunes. Nine of the large brewing companies in the St. Louis area combined to form the Independent Breweries Company. Today IBC is best known for the root beer it still makes, but in 1906, the combined might of the breweries gave the Lemp name its first serious competition in the beer market. With Billy constantly distracted by his wife, his parties, and his affairs outside of his marriage such competition he was not truly prepared for.

Advances in brewing continued to develop. What began to mar the Lemp name was the seeming indifference that Billy and the management at the Lemp Brewery seemed to show for the new and improved technology. Beer continued to be brewed the same way it had been since the refrigeration methods had moved them out of the limestone caves. For the first time, the Lemp name began to lose market share and would continue to do so throughout the first part of the new century.

Personally, 1906 was a bad year for Billy as well. His beloved mother died of cancer in April of that year. In fact, his mother died in the mansion in what is now the parlor of the William Lemp Suite. She had been diagnosed with cancer the year before, but her passing was very sudden. Billy began to truly *live it up* after his mother passed.

Billy held legendary parties. What was interesting was that he liked to hold them in the rooms beneath the mansion that had been carved out of limestone. The pool, theater, and ballroom were the places for these huge celebrations with scores of guests. William also created a bowling alley beneath the streets and amidst the limestone caves. These parties would last for days with Billy enjoying every minute.

That Lillian was aware of these parties became evident at some point. Newspaper reports that covered Lillian and William's divorce reveal some details about them. Servants stated they saw the rooms of the mansion and the caves beneath crowded with men and women. They drank. They sang. They caroused. Interestingly, it also notes that they threw chewing gum around.

Billy reportedly would bring prostitutes down into the limestone caves as well. This habit would also bring about another scandal in the Lemp family. Billy is rumored to have fathered a child with one of his affairs, either with a prostitute or one of the scores of other women he slept with. What made it worse, was that this child was born with Down Syndrome, a humiliation beyond just having a child out of wedlock at the time.

Using his vast wealth, Billy made sure no official record of this illegitimate son would exist. Only stories from servants seem to provide any proof that this sad child ever lived. Inflicting the harshest punishment he could against something he himself was responsible for, William had this child locked in the attic of the mansion. He became known as the "Monkey-Faced Boy" and was often seen by neighbors peering out the windows at the streets below. He lived in that attic until he reached the age of thirty when he died from unknown causes.

Billy seemed to grow bored with his attractive wife. His parties and dalliances became more frequent. He spent less and less time at home. He made unreasonable demands, such as telling his wife she had an allowance of $1,000 a day and had to spend all of it. If there was any left by the end of the day, then she would be cut off completely. It was only a matter of time before the marriage would end and it was actually Billy who filed for divorce.

Despite having a child, William J. Lemp III, Billy had tired of his trophy wife and wanted out of the marriage. It was 1908, a time when divorce was still something of a major scandal. The media of the time crowded the courtroom, and details of the divorce were spread throughout the country. Each story and detail was written for the public to read. It was truly a media circus and it has to stand as one of the most vicious divorces the public had ever seen. Accusations flew from both William and Lillian. They sparred over money, and they sparred most viciously over the custody of their son.

Reading newspaper accounts of the time are rather like reading some of the tabloids today. Lillian would make an accusation of parties and womanizing. William would counter with attacks against Lillian and dismiss her accusation out of hand one at a time. Each testified against the other for days at a time, only to sit on the stand again to counter accusations made. Servants and friends were called for both Lillian and William to describe debauchery and supposed evidence of someone being ill-fit to be a parent. Despite her poise throughout, a photo of Lillian smoking a cigarette in public nearly cost her custody of her son. Such things were the realm of prostitutes, and ladies did not smoke or drink in public like that.

Lillian accused her husband of things such as excessive drinking and keeping the company of other women. William countered with accusations of Lillian drinking and smoking in public. Only when a servant who was close to Lillian testified, saying she found the hairs of strange women in William's bathroom, was any shred of dignity saved for Lillian. Lillian took to abandoning her lavender clothes and wearing black during the divorce proceedings.

There was a second trial just two years after the divorce trial and this one was over the custody of William J. Lemp III, their only child. Lillian struck first by insisting that Billy not have any claim to custody over the child. She claimed that Billy was cruel to animals among other accusations of cruelty. It was another bitter fight, and Lillian ended up with custody over William III and then vanished from public life.

After the dust had settled and custody matters worked out to both parties' satisfaction, William turned his attention again to running the brewery. In 1911, he turned the mansion into the main offices for the Lemp brewery. The front section of the mansion was remodeled to contain offices and lobbies, and rooms for clerks and paperwork and bookkeepers. Still the family fortunes continued to decline. William's attention could not remain focused on one thing for very long.

Billy built a country home for himself on a bluff that overlooked the Meramec River. He dubbed the home "Alswel" in an optimistic gesture that everything would be all right now that the divorce was over. He remarried in 1915 to the daughter of a brewer named Casper Koehler. His second wife's name was Ellie. As with much in Billy's life, this happiness was short-lived.

In modern day life, it would seem as if Billy suffered from some kind of bi-polar disorder. He would have these extended periods of partying, activity, and boundless energy followed by long periods of disinterest, depression, and boredom. His life in the country pleased him for a while, as had his parties and Lillian, but eventually, the world out-paced him and he lost interest in the business.

The family fortunes declined. Other breweries were just as capable of producing more beer and then distributing it more efficiently than the Lemps. Billy seemed to show no interest in upgrading equipment in the brewery. He spent more and more time away in the country. By the time World War I came along, the once powerful Lemp brewery was a mere shadow of itself, and the brewery was just barely able to survive.

Despite the financial troubles for the brewery, Billy was still very wealthy. Just before Prohibition came into effect, the Lemp fortune was estimated at about $7 million in early 1900s money. The Lemps were still one of the richest families in St. Louis.

The final blow to the Lemp brewing dynasty seemed to come when the government passed Prohibition into law. At first, Billy seemed surprised that it had passed. Once again, he seemed to have no interest in what was going on in the world around him. He held out hope that the amendment would be overturned. Other brewers turned to brewing other things and other methods of making money. But it seemed as if the Lemps had no desire to do this. All of the relatives had enough money already—they need not work again. William's brother, Charles and Edwin, had left the brewing industry years prior. When it became obvious that Prohibition was likely to stick around for a while, Billy lost all interest in the business and closed down the brewery. This took the workers at the brewery by surprise and most of them only learned of it when they showed up for work and found the gates locked.

In 1920, tragedy struck the Lemps when Billy's sister, Elsa, followed in the family tradition. On the morning of March 20, she put a revolver to her head and pulled the trigger. She had been having marriage troubles and abdominal pains. When Billy and his brothers were called to Elsa's home, they saw no evidence of foul play.

Billy set about selling off the assets of the brewery. He sold the Falstaff name to brewer Joseph Griesedieck for $25,000 in 1922. He sold the brewery buildings and equipment to the International Shoe Company for a mere $588,000. Considering just a few years before it was worth $7 million, that was quite a sale.

Billy's partying days seemed to end once the brewery was shut down. Though he still held out hope that Prohibition would end, he retreated more and more to his country home. It was then that he began to exhibit some of the same signs his father had when he neared the end of his life. Billy became nervous, erratic, and withdrawn. He tried desperately to stay out of public life and began complaining of being sick all of the time.

On December 29, 1922, the next Lemp fell. Billy entered the mansion and stood in the area just inside the front door that was used as an office. He had a desk there and he sat down at it. He made a call to his wife, who was not at the mansion at the time. Once he finished, he opened his desk drawer and took out a .38 caliber revolver and opened his vest. He shot himself twice in the heart. He was fifty-five.

Billy left no note but, according to authorities, his son said he feared that something like that was coming. However, others who still kept in touch with Billy were not so sure. Billy had seemed in relatively high spirits, considering how moody he had been as of late. He spoke of selling the rest of the Lemp assets, like land that he still owned and some saloon locations that were still under his control. He had even put his estate in suburban Webster Groves on the market and talked about touring Europe once the sale was complete. Exactly why he chose that day to end everything will probably never be known to anyone but Billy.

Three Lemps had now committed suicide with two of those happening right in the mansion. Billy's funeral was held in the mansion itself. Billy's body was interred in the family mausoleum in Bellefontaine Cemetery. His crypt rests just above his sister Elsa's.

Chapter Five:
The Wealthy Heiress

The story of Billy's sister, Elsa, is a very short one. Again, in keeping with the times, it wasn't the women who were expected to inherit and run the family business. Elsa was expected to look pretty, attract a man, marry, and then settle down, producing more male Lemp heirs. This is a duty Elsa seems to have taken to heart.

In typical fashion for the Lemps, however, Elsa's story did not go exactly as planned. Things seemed to be going well when she married Thomas Wright in 1910. She was now the richest heiress in St. Louis. That should have been the end of her tale entirely except that her marriage was not a "happily ever after." Rather, it was an unsteady one and in December 1918, the couple separated.

When the new year came around, Elsa filed a petition for divorce. She claimed that her spouse had ceased loving her some time ago. Accusing Thomas of being cold and indifferent towards her, she claimed he was seldom at home and did everything he could to be away from her. Elsa's divorce had the potential of being as explosive as her brother Billy's, but this apparently was not the case. Elsa did not go into any more specifics about what Thomas had done to her. She made no accusations of cheating or parties or abuse. She seemed merely to have felt neglected. This did not make for headlines as sensational as those her brother and sister-in-law were generating.

Things seemed to turn around for the couple in 1920. They reconciled and were actually remarried on March 8, 1920, in New York City. When they finally made it back to St. Louis on March 19th, they found their home crammed with flowers and congratulations sent by friends. As of that night, everything seemed to be going well. That would last only until the next day.

Elsa had been complaining for a long time of abdominal problems. These pains never seemed to have been explained by doctors of the day. The pain was so intense that Elsa would often sink into an intense depression. These bouts of depression caused her to withdraw from the public eye and caused her to be restless and unable to sleep. It appears that the night her and her newly remarried husband returned to St. Louis was a bad night for her, as far as her stomach was concerned.

According to reports from her husband, Elsa was awake most of the night complaining of the stomach pain and nothing seemed to help. She tossed and turned. By the next morning, Elsa had finally managed to get to sleep. Her husband awoke and checked on her. Elsa spoke to him, saying she felt better, but was very tired. She wanted to stay in bed a while longer and rest some more. Thomas declared that this was a fine idea and that he would let her rest. He also indicated he would go down the hall and run his bath.

While Thomas was in the bathroom bathing, he heard a sharp, loud sound from the area where his wife's bedroom was. It was a sound he did not associate with gunfire. He figured his wife had gotten out of bed and then dropped something, or that she was making noise to try and get his attention. He grew concerned.

Thomas emerged from the bathroom and called to his wife. He received no response. He walked down the hall and knocked on her door. Again, there was no response. He opened the door and saw her sitting in her bed, apparently staring at him. He spoke to her. It was then that he realized something was horribly wrong. Stepping into the room, he saw her hand beside her body with the revolver still clutched in the fingers. There was blood oozing from the wound in her temple. She was still alive when he'd entered the room and she appeared to be trying to speak to him. But she never did, and she died moments later.

Despite the servants in the house, none of them were present when Elsa killed herself. None of them could think of a reason why she would want to kill herself. Everything appeared to be going right for her for a change. She left no note explaining her actions.

There were some strange actions taken by Elsa's husband after discovering her body. He first called a Dr. M. B. Clopton who came over to view the body. Then a family friend was called. Then the Circuit Attorney Lawrence McDaniel was called, and it was only when he contacted the coroner's office, that the Coroner was officially notified of Elsa's death. The police were not called for nearly two hours after her death.

The authorities did seem to think that it was strange that Thomas had waited so long to call them. The only excuse he could give was that he was so in shock that he was confused about what to do. The police made note that Thomas became highly agitated and nervous under questioning. Still, Thomas was not arrested and no charges were ever filed against him.

Despite these strange activities, it appeared as if no one in the Lemp family accused Thomas of foul play. Billy and Edwin, Elsa's brothers, were notified and they arrived at the house. It was while entering the house that Billy was heard to make the comment, "Well, that's the Lemp family for you."

Elsa passes out of this story quietly at this time. Her body was interred at the family mausoleum in Bellefontaine Cemetery.

The sign outside the Elsa Lemp Suite.

Chapter Six:
The Monkey-Faced Boy

Worthy of his own short entry in the description of the Lemp family is the illegitimate son of Billy Lemp. Of all of the stories of the Lemps, despite the suicides, it could be this Lemp story that is the saddest. Even his name has been lost to history and he has become known as the "Monkey-Faced Boy."

The exact origin of this man is not known. Billy had numerous affairs and parties where prostitutes were plentiful. It has been theorized that The Monkey-Faced Boy was born from a prostitute. What *is* known is that no record of the birth of this child exists. Again, how this came about is not entirely known. Billy was one of the richest men in St. Louis and what he wanted, he generally got. Erasing the existence of this child seemed to be something well within the realm of his power and reach.

It appears that servants are where the stories of the existence of this child come from. There have been numerous books written about haunted areas of St. Louis and they, inevitably, include the Lemp Mansion. Servants have confirmed the existence of this boy. They have confirmed that he suffered from what we now call Down Syndrome. They have confirmed that he was treated in the most horrible ways possible. He was locked away in a prison of luxury, but still a prison.

Legend has it that the attic became the place where this child lived. He was confined there for his entire life, legend also says. Stories grew around the neighborhood, from other children, who claimed to see the face of this boy peering from the tiny attic windows. It was the neighborhood children, upon seeing the face of a Down Syndrome boy, who dubbed him, even then The Monkey-Faced Boy.

Imagine what is must have been like. Exactly how mentally disabled this boy was is unknown. Since he seems to have had no formal education, he probably never had the chance to develop much at all. He would not understand why he was confined to one room of this large house. He would not understand why no one would talk to him. He would not understand why he could not play with the children he could only watch from the windows of his prison day after day after day.

Whether or not Billy showed any affection to this child can only be guessed. Given Billy's personality and judging from his actions with his spouses, his moodiness, his fits of depression, and his ultimate withdrawal from life, it is probably safe to say Billy thought as little about this child as he could. This was a constant reminder of his failures.

The hallway in the haunted attic.

Pictures of the attic show a relatively large space as far as width goes. The ceiling is somewhat low. The windows are curving in nature and set very low to the floor. The boy would have to sit on the floor to look out.

This forgotten child lived until the age of thirty. For those years, his existence can only be imagined. It must have been one of complete and profound loneliness. The circumstances of his death are not even known, but it is probably a safe bet that he was not given the kind of medical care that would have been afforded a child who was legitimate and who did not have Down Syndrome. With no friends, a father who probably preferred to imagine he did not exist, and a family who agreed with that prospect, it must have been a sad life and one of total isolation.

The circumstances around his death are also not known. It is known only that this sad creature lived until the age of thirty and died in the mansion. He had managed to outlive the father that never wanted him in the first place. His existence was then, finally, erased permanently.

Only one tangible piece of evidence exists that would seem to indicate that this boy ever lived. At the Lemp plot in Bellefontaine Cemetery, there is a marker. It has no dates and bears only the family name in bold letters: LEMP. It is believed that this, as sad as things were for him in life, is his sad resting place in death.

Chapter Seven:
The Family Curse

Charles Lemp had worked in the brewery, like his brothers, for a very short time when he was young. However, running a beer company did not seem exactly like Charles' cup of tea. He left the family business to pursue his own interests.

Charles Lemp pursued his own business and he developed an interest in politics. He went into the banking field and was very successful. The combination of personal wealth, family name, and his dabblings in politics kept Charles in the public eye, despite his attempts to remove himself from it.

By all accounts, Charles was a bit of a strange man. He was very private and grew more reclusive the older he got. Whether this was the simple Lemp mental illness as it had always presented itself or perhaps some concern over the family history pressing down on him, cannot be known for certain.

What *is* known is that Charles had moved away from the mansion and the brewery and started a life away from his family when his brother, William, killed himself. Charles came into possession of the family fortune and the mansion when William died. His brother, Edwin, urged him to sell the place, but Charles seemed to suddenly grow an interest in the place he had tried hard to get away from.

Charles settled in and began to renovate the mansion yet again. This time the mansion was being turned back in a residence. Charles seemed to develop an attachment to the home, and once the renovations were complete, he moved back into the house. Charles lived alone, with only two servants as company, feeding the rumors about his sanity.

Refusing to leave the mansion, Charles lived year after year in the place as the house itself began to crumble around him. He seemed to show little interest in keeping up appearances.

His brother, Edwin, appeared to show some concern over his brother's health. He urged his brother, repeatedly, to move out of the house. Given the history of the place, Edwin probably had some justification of his worry. Instead, Charles seemed more adamant than ever to stay in the house. He grew increasingly withdrawn.

Charles continued to putter around his dusty and crumbling mansion for a number of years, growing increasingly strange. At some point, he got a dog which he was apparently quite fond of—a Doberman Pinscher. Beyond that, his servants, and some communications with his brother, Charles seemed to have cut himself off from the world as he reached his seventies.

At some point, Charles made out his will and made very detailed funeral arrangements. He did not want to be interred in the family mausoleum with the rest of his siblings. He wanted his body to be taken to the Missouri Crematory and reduced to ashes immediately upon his body being found. He ordered that his body was not to be bathed or changed or even put in clothes. He was not to have a funeral service and there was to be no death notice published for him in the newspaper. Apparently, his desire for isolation extended into his afterlife. He also stated that these orders were to be followed no matter what any surviving family members said to the contrary.

These orders were written many years before Charles finally succumbed to the Lemp Family Curse. He was seventy-seven years old on May 10, 1949. He had become very afraid of germs and was terrified of touching people by that time. He was alone in the house that night. Using the same type of gun his relatives had, a .38 caliber revolver, Charles shot his beloved Doberman Pinscher. Although he shot the dog in the basement, the dog's body was found on the stairs leading to the second floor. He then went up to his room, climbed into bed and shot himself in the head.

Of all of the suicides in the family, only Charles bothered to leave a note. It gave no details as to why he felt it was time to end his life. His note read simply, "In case I am found dead, blame it on no one but me."

His intentions were followed to the letter. His body was cremated. His brother, Edwin, picked up the remains from the funeral home and buried his brother on Charles' farm. An interesting side note to that is that, even to this day, no evidence exists to show where Charles' farm ever was, so exactly where his remains may be now is unknown.

Even though he tried hard earlier in his life to leave behind the Lemp family, he ended up becoming very much a part of the family's history. He would also become part of the family's future along with his brother William, William's illegitimate son, and William's wife, Lillian. It seems that Charles' love for the mansion extended even past his death.

Chapter Eight:
The Remaining Lemps

This leaves the story with two remaining Lemps whose tales have yet to be told, with each of their lives and subsequent deaths standing apart from the rest of the family simply by how relatively mundane they were. One in particular, the much fought-for son of Billy, died in a way that was tragic and yet remarkably uneventful. The final son, Edwin, had his share of the Lemp family madness towards the end of his life, but he managed to break the curse for the most part.

William Lemp III pretty much vanished from public life after the tumultuous divorce that his mother and father played out in public and through the national media of the time. Other than showing up again in the newspaper as his mother and father fought over custody of him, his life was pretty much an unknown and apparently rather unremarkable. Much like his mother, once he was out of the orbit of the Lemps brewery, his life was not worth taking note of, it seems. There are no indications that William Lemp III followed in his father's footsteps into the rich playboy role that he'd played to the hilt. Of course, by the time he had reached the age when he would normally have fallen under his father's wing to take over the business, Billy had mostly run the Lemp business into the ground. Therefore, there was no brewing business for William III to learn. He was wealthy because he was a Lemp, but he did not set out into politics or set forth into business like his Uncle Charles.

What *is* known is that William III died young, but not in a way that was violent or dramatic. In 1943, at the age of forty-two, William III died of a heart attack. He was not at the mansion. He soon joined the rest of his family in the cemetery.

With the death of his nephew, the only remaining Lemp was Edwin. Edwin was very similar to his brother, Charles, in that he had no desire to go into the family business. He'd probably worked in the brewery as a young man much like his brother had. However, Edwin did not want to work in the brewing business, either before or after Prohibition. He moved out to neighboring Kirkwood, Missouri, a suburb of St. Louis, bought an estate there, and managed his money.

Edwin appears to have lived a very secluded life. When his brothers and other relatives died, he was truly alone. He lived with servants on his estate, but he had no more family. He apparently never married, nor had any children. He became, as he got older, obsessed with living alone and often invited friends to stay at his home.

Despite this, Edwin shunned publicity. He turned down offers to speak about family, their fortunes, the mansion, and their tragic deaths. He did not talk about them. He did not mention them. He accumulated priceless works of art and Lemp family documents, and then kept them to himself in his estate in Kirkwood.

Edwin became fanatical about keeping someone with him at all times. It seems his family's history weighed upon him. He was determined not to give into the supposed curse of the Lemp family. He managed his money so well that he did not have to work or explore other options in business. He was able to live through the Depression without any ill effects.

Edwin succeeded in his goal of breaking the family curse. He lived a very long, if very lonely, life in Kirkwood. He was seen as rather eccentric, but not particularly crazy. He lived until the age of ninety and passed away quietly of natural causes in 1970.

With the death of Edwin Lemp, the Lemp line was broken permanently. There would be no more Lemps to inherit the family fortune. In fact, Edwin made sure that much information about the family would be destroyed upon his death. He left strict orders that all of his priceless works of art and the valuable historical Lemp documents be destroyed. A butler accommodated his wishes and burned all of the documents, art, and artifacts in a giant bonfire. Whatever secrets Edwin may have been hiding in his house in the suburbs, went up in a blaze.

Johann Lemp probably died thinking that his family and their legacy were set for all time. He probably died convinced that his family would be cared for and that there would be a nearly endless line of descendents throughout history. He may have even had ideas that the Lemp name would be tied with successful brewing in the United States for all time.

The truth ended up being something quite different—lives of tragedy and scandal and mental illness. What ended up happening was a life of headlines and sensational deaths. What happened was a legacy of suicide and a large mansion reputed to be haunted. In just under a century, a family had reached the highest heights of wealth and power that this country had to offer, only to lose it all and vanish entirely from the planet less than 100 years later.

The story of the Lemps, however, did not end with the death of Edwin. No, the most sensational stories were yet to come for this family. The stories were to surround something that had become a part of the Lemp family. The stories were to circulate around the Lemp Mansion itself.

Chapter Nine:
The Mansion

It is has been said that houses have personalities. It has also been said that houses can live and breathe. It is also commonly believed that houses and homes take on the personality of the people who lived in them. If that is the case, then the Lemp Mansion has well-deserved its reputation.

The history of the house has been discussed previously because the history of the house is so tied with the family who owned it. The history of the Lemp Mansion is entwined with the history the Lemp family, and the two cannot be separated. The mansion's changes, expansions, and reductions seem to have mirrored the psychoses of the person in the family who owned it at the time. It expanded under Billy's manic phases and then was reduced to something more manageable under Charles' more moody years.

The reason the mansion itself becomes such a character of the Lemp family is that the mansion was one of the most outward symbols of their power and their wealth. It was built and constructed during William Lemp, Sr.'s years to be a showplace for Victorian elegance. However, as the Lemps declined it was the mansion that still showed the world this family had money and some sort of power.

However, it was the only thing connected with the Lemps that continued to live and grow and become something beyond the story of a family entrenched in tragedy after the last Lemp passed away. It is the mansion that still stands today and still tells its tales. The mansion is, then, the only true living Lemp.

Even the birth of this stately manor is shrouded with a bit with mystery. It was William Lemp, Sr.'s father-in-law, Jacob Freickert, who originally built it. While the land and mansion was in Jacob's name, it is largely believed that it was Lemp money that financed the purchase and constructions. While Jacob was not financially destitute, the size of the mansion, even at its early stages, was large enough that money from the Lemp empire was probably needed to build the home. It is commonly believed that William himself financed the construction of the mansion.

Of course, location was key as well. The mansion was a very short distance from the brewery. The same caves that were being used to brew beer were underneath the mansion. Even in the early days, the idea of using rooms in the mansion for extra brewery offices was considered.

The mansion was impressive even as Jacob finished construction, fully constructed in 1868 and then purchased outright by William in 1876. No sooner had the ink dried on the deal, and William was busy making his home even more impressive and an even bigger show of his family's wealth.

William spent his money lavishly and turned the home into the aforementioned Victorian showplace. The mansion, once William was done, had thirty-three rooms. While it was not a sprawling house, it was one that was rather tall, covered with windows from ground to attic. It had buildings behind it for horses and servants. At the time it was first built, there was not much around it in terms of a neighborhood, and it stood out to passers-by as an impressive piece of architecture and a true show of wealth.

William also had built three room-sized walk-in vaults. Each vault measured out at thirteen feet high, fifteen feet wide and twenty-five feet deep. William Sr. was also the one who oversaw the construction below the mansion, including the tunnel that connected the mansion to the brewery.

Walled-off entrance to the tunnels.

As has been mentioned before, the world beneath the ground of the mansion sets the story of this house apart from so many others. While other houses in other parts of the country may have had tunnels for nefarious or noble purposes, the Lemps seemed to have built an underground world because they could, and they had the money to do it. To this day, there are steps leading down to the limestone caves beneath the mansion, but they end in a metal grate. The staff of the Lemp Mansion refer to this gate, affectionately, as "The Gates of Hell."

It is beneath the mansion that Billy descended into his life of debauchery, adultery, and partying. Beneath the mansion are the heated limestone pool, natural auditorium, bowling alley, and ballroom. Each room is carved out of the hardest limestone. Each room remains a steady sixty degrees all year around. The auditorium still has a stage and faded sets. The sets were made out of cardboard and other cheap materials and the stage was lit with crude stage lights. The seats were carved out of the limestone as well providing adequate, if uncomfortable, seating.

Billy and Lillian took over the mansion after William Senior ended his own life. It was Billy who ran from the brewery offices when summoned by servants who heard the gunshot to the mansion. It was Billy who ran up the stairs and kicked down the door to his father's room. It was Billy who first found his father's body with the smoking revolver still clutched in his hand.

Billy set about putting his own mark on the mansion. He liked the most expensive things. Billy lived a life of luxury and was, in most respects, a spoiled rich kid. He was used to getting what he wanted and never knew a day of actual hard work or struggle. Lillian came from a rich family as well. She was beautiful, he was handsome, and they were the toast of the town. The two of them began spending the family fortune as fast as they could.

Billy did not start out doing additional construction on the house. No, he seemed determined just to fill it with every luxury he could get his hands on. When he and Lillian were living in the mansion, they spent money lavishly on servants and works of art. They bought expensive carriages and Lillian had her horse's tackle dyed her favorite color of Lavender. Each of them stocked their closets with more clothing than any couple should really need, and all of it was the most expensive of the time.

The fact that his partying ways eventually caught up with him seemed to put the brakes on Billy. He had to deal with his illegitimate son and now the mansion's attic came into play. It was turned into a kind of ostentatious prison for a child no one wanted to admit even existed. The sad windows overlooked the parks and places where the other neighborhood children played and from those glass eyes, the Monkey-Faced Boy would be seen looking.

The divorce that played out so publicly and dragged the family's shame into the open further took the wind out of Billy's sails. No sooner had the divorce been finalized and the custody dispute settled, then Prohibition set in. Before reaching that point, however, Billy seemed to take a renewed interest in the business and decided to remodel the mansion.

Billy remodeled the front of the mansion, creating radical changes in the appearance of the mansion. He turned the mansion into the new offices of the Lemp brewing empire, converted the front part of the home into offices for clerks and secretaries and added lobbies and private offices. Billy's own private office was located on the first floor, and it was in this office that he pointed a gun at his own chest and fired into it twice.

The Lemp Mansion also stood as a kind of living and visible example of the decline of the Lemp family. The house began to decline once the fortunes of the family also began to decline with the advent of Prohibition. Charles Lemp took over the mansion at this point and he converted the home back into a living space and removed the offices and clerk rooms. He removed the lobbies and began to use the home as it had originally been intended to be used.

Charles Lemp was a man who lived a very solitary life. He lived in the home with two servants and the illegitimate son of his brother Billy. Charles was living there when the Monkey-Faced Boy died mysteriously at the age of thirty. Around the mansion, the neighborhood that surrounded the home began to change as well.

Like most cities, the downtown areas of St. Louis began to change. Namely, people started moving away from the urban areas and into the suburbs. The Lemp Mansion was not far from downtown and was very urban. The affluent who used to live there moved away. The houses around the mansion began to decline. As Charles Lemp sat behind his walls, the house he lived in began to decline along with the neighborhood. Charles seemed to have little interest in maintaining the house.

During the 1960s, a large portion of the mansion's grounds was taken away for the building of Interstate 55. The once lavish grounds were much shorter. The mansion itself was a mere shadow of what it once was.

After Charles Lemp died, the mansion was turned into a boarding house. Considering the way Charles lived in the mansion, stories were already starting to circulate about the place being haunted. Whenever you have a prominent family with that big of a house and that many suicides occurring there, then you will have talking. This was a house that would not stay silent.

The boarding house idea did not work very well for the Lemp Mansion. Stories arose telling of noises that were heard in the middle of the night. People were uncomfortable staying there. The owners could not make any money. So, the house was essentially abandoned, and it looked like the Lemp Mansion was going to become just another piece of urban decay.

In 1975, a man by the name of Dick Pointer and his family stepped in and rescued the mansion. He must have figured it was pointless to fight the history and the legends surrounding the building, so why not use it to promote the place. The building was saved, the grounds were redone, and the home was turned into a dinner theater, restaurant, and, most importantly, a bed and breakfast. It remains a popular bed and breakfast to this day.

The Lemp Mansion is decorated with period pieces and furniture. Much of the former glory of the place has been restored. Paintings of the family members hang along the walls. Newspaper stories are placed in the rooms that detail the history of the place, including the unnatural deaths of Lemps at their own hands. Even the attic is accessible by the public.

The inn is made up of four suites. Each suite is named after a family member. There is even a Lavender room named after the ex-wife of Billy and after her nickname, "The Lavender Lady."

These days, word of the Lemp Mansion has spread enough that the restaurant and rooms are often used for weddings and receptions. The food at the restaurant is highly praised. The rooms are seldom empty. It seems that people come to the mansion hoping to experience something that they cannot explain. The owner has stated that he is very lucky, because it certainly seems like they are rarely disappointed.

They say houses are never silent. They say that houses live and they breathe. They say some houses are born bad. There are a lot of sayings about houses. The Lemp Mansion is a house full of history. It is a house full of stories. It seems that the Lemp Mansion has not yet finished telling its stories.

Part Two:
The Alternate History

This is where things get a little strange. You see, there is another history of the house. This is the history that the people who lived there have told *certain people*. The part that's strange is that much of this story was told *after* the main characters were long dead.

Most of this story was told to me and a group of people who signed up to take a tour of the Lemp Mansion. Not everyone on the tour was spending the night there. I was. So were three friends of mine. So were four other people who became friends that night.

The woman who lead the tour was a woman named Betsy. Betsy is a woman with a theatrical flair. She is entertaining. She can tell a story. She is very convincing. She knows her stuff. She talks to ghosts.

Betsy has been talking to the ghosts that walk and live in the Lemp Mansion for a long time now. She and her partners do a lot of spirit work in the St. Louis area, but the Lemp Mansion is a particular favorite. The Lemp Mansion is the one that allows the most access. The Lemp Mansion has some of the most talkative ghosts, evidently.

So Betsy tells us the story of the family and the mansion. The story she tells, however, is different from the story I have been researching. She has a different take on Billy Lemp, for example. She also has more to tell us about William Lemp's wife, Julia. Finally, she has an entirely different story for the poor deformed "Monkey-Faced Boy."

Is what she told me the truth? Can she be believed? I can't say for sure. Even if she can do what she says she can do, can the spirits involved be believed? Who can truly know that?

I do know that while I was with this woman, I experienced some things I have never experienced again. I even may have contacted a spirit or two on my own. I will leave the truth or the falseness of everything for you to decide. I will simply start by telling you what Betsy told me about the Lemp family. Then I can tell you about the ghosts who lurk in this remarkable house—and about my own visit there.

Chapter Ten:
Fathers and Sons

The story from Betsy about Billy Lemp is a little bit different than the tales told as common knowledge. Betsy claims that Billy is her favorite spirit to talk to, but admits that he is not the type of person she would necessarily want to know in the real world. She states that Billy, in fact, made an effort to be a good son, but it was his father who broke Billy's heart.

According to Betsy, Billy has informed her that he studied hard to learn the family business. He went to school and trained to become a master brewer. He studied the ins and outs of the brewing business. Since he was the oldest, he assumed that all of his studying and work and learning would mean that he would be the chosen son. Billy assumed the family business would be handed to him naturally.

As the tale goes and is known by history, this did not happen. Billy was told by his father that he wasn't ready, and would never be ready, to manage the family business. Billy was crushed. He had to stand aside as his father chose his younger brother over him and made no attempt to disguise the fact that Frederick was his favorite.

This may not excuse how Billy turned out or his actions from that point, but it may explain it a little bit. Considering it was Billy who ran from the brewery to the mansion upon hearing that his father had shot himself, you have to wonder if he spent much of the rest of his life trying to prove himself worthy of the family business. Was he the type to spend the rest of his life trying to gain the love and the trust of his father?

The other father/son story that sounds different when you talk to Betsy is that of Billy Lemp and the "Monkey-Faced Boy." She has a whole different take on this—that she claims comes directly from Billy. She says that not only does this person have a name, but that he wasn't the bastard son of Billy and some nameless and unknown prostitute.

According to Betsy, this young man's name was Zeke. He was actually Billy Lemp's brother. He lived until the age of sixteen. He was born from Julia, Billy Lemp's mother, and she had this child near the age of fifty. Her advanced age caused the boy to be born deformed. The nature of his deformity is evidently unknown even to Betsy and her conversations with the spirits in the mansion.

As for why this young man was kept in the attic well, again, according to Betsy, that was for his own safety. Whatever his disability was, he needed almost constant watching and care. The servant's quarters were on the third floor or attic of the mansion. There were caretakers and servants who were able to provide the constant care needed to take care of this child and to keep him safe. As to the reason why no record of this child existed is still unknown, nor why he was buried without a name.

Given Betsy's talents, it is hard to know what is real and what isn't. She says there are seven spirits in the mansion, and five of those are members of the Lemp family. Having regular contact with them, she has tried to help them in this plane of existence.

Betsy has some interesting insight into the hauntings at the Lemp. So, it is at this time that we should discuss the occurrences and the things that have been reported in this amazing house. Whether or not you believe that the house is haunted is up to you. What I can say is that there are strange things going on at the house that is now a restaurant, dinner theater, and a bed and breakfast.

Chapter Eleven: A Different Take on the Mansion

According to the tale told by Betsy, the mansion was not one commissioned by William Lemp. According to the tale she tells, it was the residence of William's father-in-law. The Feickert's lived in the home as their own. They invited William over one night, and William met their daughter, Julia. It was love at first sight. When the two married, they actually moved in with Julia's parents.

Eventually, the house was turned over to William, however, and he did go about doing some massive remodeling. At one time, the top of the mansion had a widow's walk that was later torn down. The circular room near the back, that is now referred to as "The Jungle Room," was originally made of nearly all glass. Even the roof of this building was made of glass. This was a room constructed for Julia who loved nature and animals. It's hard to imagine when you look at the neighborhood as it is now, but at one time it was an area of hills and fields. There were no houses surrounding the Lemp Mansion save for the DeMenil mansion which was next door. Julia would have had a view of nature all around her.

The house was remodeled again when Billy took over and he turned the place into offices. The glass roof was removed and two windows were taken out of the atrium. An office was put above the area, and that area also served as a nursery at times.

The area that is now the bar once served as the Lemp Library. When Charles Lemp became ill, it was converted into his bedroom. Again, Betsy has a different tale than the common history. It is in this room, on the first floor, where she says Charles Lemp shot himself. However, a plaque on the Charles Lemp Suite on the second floor indicates that it is there where it is believed he killed himself. Betsy makes no mention of Charles' dog ending up anywhere but where Charles reputedly shot the animal, which was in the basement.

After Charles' death, the mansion entered its history as a boarding house. According to Betsy, it became a flophouse. At one time, eighteen families, not just individuals, but families, lived in the mansion. The huge, beautiful parlor that is just inside the front door was chopped in half and made into two rooms that families could live in. The beautiful frescoes that cover the ceilings of the mansion were covered with drop-down ceilings.

The mansion itself was threatened by the construction of the highway I-55. The original plans were to send the highway directly through the mansion. History would have been lost. Of course, the mansion was hardly anything to write home about—it was hardly standing. The house truly looked more like a flophouse than a glorious mansion or a Victorian ode to the days when beer barons ruled St. Louis.

The construction of the highway also threatened the DeMenil mansion right next door. Someone decided that the DeMenil mansion, only slightly older than the Lemp Mansion, should be saved. It was eventually declared a historic site and that saved it from the wrecking ball. By saving the DeMenil, the Lemp Mansion was also saved. The highway was bent around the mansions and though the Lemp estate lost a coach house and some land, the bulk of the mansion is still there.

It was the amazing insight of the Pointer family that turned the Lemp Mansion into the tourist attraction that it is today. Somehow they were able to see through the rotting drop-down ceilings to what the mansion truly was. Before it was opened to the public, again, massive remodeling occurred. The drop-down ceiling was removed. Then inches of paint were scraped away to find the amazing frescoes. The wall that divided the parlor was removed.

Somehow, despite the damage done to other parts of the house and the rotten things that must have happened within its walls when it was a flophouse, the mansions amazing African carvings in the parlor were saved. Artists were called in to restore the ceilings and re-paint the atrium. Every effort was made to make the place as Victorian-era as possible.

But the Lemp Mansion has a life all its own. Whether the spirits that reportedly reside within the walls have ever been able to influence the area around it to save the mansion can only be guessed at in this day and age. What is known is that the mansion somehow survived. Despite the decline of the neighborhood around it, the mansion still stands. Despite the progress of the city around it, the mansion still stands. Despite the decline of the mansion itself and the souls who lived and died and sweat there as it had its life as a boarding house and flophouse, the mansion still stands.

Part Three:
Restless Spirits

The thing that most people want to talk about when it comes to the Lemp Mansion is the ghosts, of course. Despite the rich history and the general beauty of such a place, people generally come and want to spend time at the mansion in the hopes of seeing something they can't explain. Even skeptics want to come in hopes of seeing something they without logical explanation, and then try hard to explain it. The interesting thing about the Lemp Mansion is they are seldom disappointed.

Life magazine, back in 1980, declared the Lemp Mansion one of the top five most haunted placed in the country. In recent years, it has moved up. A special of haunted places on the cable network *The Travel Channel* declared the Lemp Mansion number two.

When I visited the Lemp Mansion in September 2006, I went with several friends. My friends had been there numerous times before and they loved the place. While they had experienced a couple of things they couldn't explain, this time we all experienced things that left us scratching our heads and wondering. The interesting thing about the mansion, however, is that none of the legends would be there if the Lemp family itself weren't so mentally ill.

Quite obviously depression ran in the family. Billy Lemp certainly exhibited signs of frantic energy followed by deep depressions and moodiness that are the hallmarks of bi-polar disorders. Of course, the biggest sign of mental illness would be a rash of suicides. As my friend pointed out, none of us would be here at the mansion if the family itself were not mentally ill.

Still, the mansion existed well after the last Lemp passed away. When there was no longer a Lemp to live in the mansion, the life of the house continued. Dozens of souls inhabited the place when the mansion became a boarding house and then a flophouse. Some of those spirits are reputed to still reside within the opulent walls of the Lemp Mansion.

It's time to study the haunted history of the mansion, it's territory that leaves a lot up to the imaginations, and it's territory that cannot be confirmed through modern means. However, nearly everyone who has spent time at, or worked at, the Lemp Mansion has a story to tell.

Chapter Twelve:
The Haunted Place

The tales of strange things going on at the Lemp Mansion started almost immediately upon turning into a boarding house. Residents began to hear and see things that they couldn't explain. Sounds and strange sights are the most commonly discussed things talked about at the Lemp Mansion. The sounds of footsteps walking up and down the stairs and up and down the hallways where no one was visibly walking were the most common.

To go along with the footsteps, there are common reports of people having the feeling of being watched. Residents said that when they were walking about the house, they had the sensation of eyes on them and would turn to find themselves alone in a hallway or in the room. As if that wasn't enough, there are common complaints of voices in the hallway where no one was standing. Even more chilling were the reports of residents and guests hearing their own names whispered in the night over and over again.

One of the more haunted areas of the mansion is what is now considered the William Lemp Suite on the second floor and right at the top of the stairs. The common complaint is that anxious footsteps would be heard running up the stairs, and this would be followed by the sounds of someone pounding or kicking the door of the bedroom. This is believed to be Billy Lemp reenacting the time when he was summoned from the brewery, running up the stairs to reach his father after he had shot himself.

In the years as the mansion struggled to survive as a boarding-house, the owners found it more and more difficult to find tenants. As the rumors began to spread that the place was haunted, the clientele came from the lower and lower rungs of civilization. As the neighborhood deteriorated, so did the mansion, and so did the people on the inside. Despite having up to eighteen families in the place at one point, by the time the 1970s came around, the place was barely functioning and barely standing.

A man with the last name of Pointer took a look at the intricate carvings on the mantelpieces in the parlor and this helped him decide that he wanted to own the mansion and restore it. The sale of the mansion was made, but the mansion needed a lot of work. Workers were hired to begin the arduous process of turning a flophouse into a place where people would want to eat and watch theater and spend the night. The tales of strange things happening started up again.

Workers on the mansion began telling tales of their tools disappearing. They reported a constant feeling of being watched. Other workers said they heard strange noises and some stated they had seen apparitions. For many, it was too much to bear and there were workers who walked off the job in the middle of the day, never to return.

In a famous case, there was a German man hired to do some painting. One day, he simply got up, grabbed his tools and walked off, saying he would never return. He had been experiencing the feeling of eyes watching him. The final straw was when a ghostly voice whispered his name. At that point, he had had enough, and he gathered his tools and left the place, complaining that something crazy was going on in the mansion and that the place had to be haunted.

William Lemp Suite—bed and parlor.

Once the renovations were completed, the inn opened as a restaurant. Workers began reporting that glasses would fly off the bar or float through the air. Waitresses reported seeing people sitting at tables who would vanish when approached. Others who were guests at the restaurant, would see a family sitting at one of the tables who would later vanish.

Guests and employees report things like keys, knives, and coins disappearing upon being set down. Other visitors reported hearing strange noises and whispers. Doors will lock and unlock without explanation. Doors will also open and close without being touched.

The bathroom on the lower floor is historic on its own as the first free-standing shower located in St. Louis. These days, it serves as the ladies room for guests and people visiting the restaurant. Back when it was the Lemp family home, the restroom was Billy Lemp's private bathroom. Now the sink is reported to turn on by itself. Some women have also stated that they've seen the face of a man peering through the clouded windows at them while they were inside bathroom. It is believed to be the womanizing Billy stopping by to take a look.

The stairway just inside the house is reportedly one of the more haunted areas of the house. The stairway was not always a part of the house. When the house was also the offices of the brewery, the area of the stairs was actually an elevator.

Visitors have reported seeing a full apparition of a older man wearing a suit. He is often seen walking the floors and usually has a stern look on his face with the appearance of a scowl. This is rumored to be the visage of Charles Lemp.

The attic area is rumored to be one of the most haunted areas of the house. This was the supposed domain of the "Monkey-Faced Boy." Here whispers have been reported. Often, a guest's name will be whispered again and again. Some voices reportedly encourage guests to come play with whomever the voice belongs to. One of the more popular gimmicks of ghost hunters is to place some sort of toy in a circle in the attic area. Many have reported that the toy will be moved or will show to have been played with in some way.

There are guests who have not been able to stay a full night at the mansion. This may be why the mansion now has a policy of *no refunds and no cancellations.*

At least one employee, a bartender, from the mansion reports that he once spent the night in the attic. He had been trying to drive home during a snowstorm and found himself near the mansion and unable to move any further in the driving snow. He thought he would spend the night there and figured he would get into less trouble by spending it in the attic since that was rarely rented out at the time.

Employees are not actually supposed to spend the night at the mansion. He figured that by staying in the attic, he would get into less trouble if he was caught. He let himself in and crept upstairs. As the snow blew outside, he crawled into bed, and pulled the covers up to his head, falling asleep.

Somewhere in the middle of the night, he was awakened by a voice whispering his name over and over and over again. Unable to move, he willed himself to keep his eyes shut. At some point, he fell back to sleep or drifted off. As soon as he felt light on his face and opened his eyes to see morning filtering through the windows, he grabbed his shoes and ran out into snow up to his knees while still barefoot.

Not that long ago, a tour guide was standing in the room where William Lemp, Sr. had his office. She heard what sounded like horses neighing and moving about outside the window. When the guide looked, there was nothing. However, back when William had the room as his office, the location outside the window was where guests would tie up their horses.

A waitress at the restaurant once approached a man sitting near the back of the restaurant area. As she advanced, the man abruptly disappeared. This same apparition has been reported again and again.

A waitress currently working at the mansion claims that she was once walking up the stairs and her keys were knocked out of her hand. She claims that it was not merely her dropping them but that the keys flew out of her hand as though they were slapped out.

One female guest of the mansion was staying in the Charles Lemp Suite. She and her husband had gone to bed. During the night, the wife sensed movement in the room. She opened her eyes and found a man in a suit standing at the foot of her bed with his arms crossed, scowling at her. She attempted to awaken her husband but was unable to.

Another time, a couple was staying in the William Lemp Suite and had been informed by the mansion management that they were alone in the entire building. This is not uncommon, actually. Believ-

The author in Billy Lemp's office.

ing they had the place to themselves, they partied loudly and long. Both of them eventually left the room to visit the restroom down the hall. They were surprised when the door to the Charles Lemp Suite burst open and a elderly man came barreling out to glare at them. The couple was shocked and they apologized profusely.

The next morning the couple was checking out. As they gave back their keys and talked to the members of management, they said they wished to convey their apologies to the man in the other room. Puzzled the employee checked the books. Sure enough, the couple were the only ones who were scheduled to spend the night in the mansion that night.

Those are just some of the stories. Who is reputed to be wandering the halls of the Lemp Mansion? Who still resides there? How many spirits are reported to be seen and wandering the hallways and stairways and bathrooms of the inn?

Chapter Thirteen:
The Ghostly Residents

According to those who claim to be able to speak to the spirits within the walls of the Lemp Mansion, there are seven ghosts. Five of those in the mansion are supposedly members of the Lemp Family, while the other two are not. Of course, others who also claim to be experts, say there are more than that. The debate these days amongst those who believe in the existence of the spirits in the mansion is: Are all of the spirits friendly or has something more sinister moved in?

Billy Lemp is reputed to be one of the most active spirits. It is supposedly Billy who charges up the stairs to pound on his father's bedroom door much as he did when he heard the news of his father's suicide. It is Billy who reportedly is spotted in the first floor ladies restroom peeking in on the women using the stalls or running the water in the sink. Billy supposedly likes the women who visit the mansion, and even among some of the women who report to be able to speak to spirits, Billy is one of their favorites. He also likes to reside in the room where he shot himself.

Charles Lemp is the spirit who likes to make his full presence known. Charles likes to appear almost as though he were there in the flesh. He has a kind of guardian-like feel to him. Some believe that the reason he came back to the mansion, when others wanted him to sell it, was due to his guardian-like nature and over a feeling of safe-guarding the history of his family. Charles also wanders the hall with the spirit of his dog. He is often described as an older man dressed in an old-fashioned suit with a very sour look on his face. Apparently Charles approves of little of what is now going on in his former home.

Julie Lemp is a spirit that seems to not understand that she is dead and has no conception of what is going on around her. Julia is an apparition that is seen wandering up and down the halls of the mansion looking for her children. She is apparently very interested in one particular child and that would be one of the spirits that reportedly still haunts the mansion today.

Zeke Lemp is the one who is known to most as the "Monkey-Faced Boy." Of all of the spirits, it is Zeke's who may be the most active and the most talked about. Zeke's territory is the attic where he spent his life, but the room that supposedly is visited the most by Zeke is now the Elsa Lemp Suite. The area behind this room used to be Zeke's playroom, and he evidently still likes to play there. It is Zeke who allegedly whispers the names of guests and workers. It is Zeke who likes to play with toys left out by the ghost-hunters and guests.

As for the fifth member of the Lemp family who still wanders the halls of the mansion there is some debate. Records show people claiming they see a ghostly woman wearing lavender wandering the halls and the gardens. Others claim to smell the scent of lavender when they enter or leave a room. While others maintain that the members of the Lemp family that are still wandering the halls are more of the animal variety. Charles Lemp's dog reportedly wanders the halls not far from its master's side. Others claim to run into ghostly cats or other dogs that were kept as pets by Julia Lemp.

Another spirit that purportedly wanders the hall is a former caretaker for the mansion. She supposedly has a fondness for children and taking care of them. She is seen drifting through the halls and wandering in and out of rooms. She is rumored to be a kind and gentle spirit and not one likely to stir up trouble or cause problems for the people who stay there.

The final spirit mentioned is a little girl. This spirit has been reported by the ghost-hunter Betsy who also, as mentioned prior, claims to be able to speak to the spirits there. She says that she knew there was a little girl in the house and that something had happened to this girl that caused her to die young and violently. But no records of the mansion showed any little girl ever being murdered in the house. Betsy states this is a girl from the time when the Lemp Mansion was a boardinghouse and she was a resident.

Upstairs hallway of the Mansion.

According to Betsy, this little girl's name is Sarah. She says that Sarah died brutally. Betsy also claims that the spirit of Charles Lemp witnessed this violent death and now Sarah and Charles walk near each other in the after-life. Despite his scowl, evidently Charles has a soft spot for kids.

Of course, it's one thing to read about and hear about these supposed spirits and what they do. It's another to see things firsthand. However, to truly tell the story of the Lemp Mansion one needs to see mansion. Even better, when telling the story of the Lemp Mansion, it would be better if the person doing the telling spent the night there. Better than that would be if the person doing the telling witnessed something that he or she couldn't explain.

That's exactly what I did. I knew that in order to tell the story of the Lemps and their mansion I would need to sit in their house. I would need to sleep in a bed. I would need to see if the spirits would want to come around and tell me their story.

Chapter Fourteen:
A Night in the Lemp Mansion

The Lemp mansion sits just across I-55 from the Anheuser-Busch brewery. I-55 nearly goes right through the mansion and, in fact, nearly did go right through the mansion if not for a few maneuverings that prevented that a long time ago. If you have plans of going to St. Louis and you have an interest in ghosts, hauntings, old mansions or historical sites, you need to visit this location. It is a restaurant, so you can eat lunch or dinner there. There is a dinner theater that I hear is a lot of fun. Finally, it is a bed and breakfast—and that is the experience I took advantage of.

This is where I met the wonderful woman, Betsy, spoken of earlier. It is she who conducts ghost tours of the mansion on Monday nights. I highly recommend you visit this attraction of the Lemp mansion. At the time of this writing, the tour charges a fee of $15 and, in my opinion, worth every penny. Because Betsy is a woman who claims to be clairvoyant and able to talk to spirits, she does a lot of work at, by all accounts, haunted places around St. Louis—and conducts tours with many of them. The Lemp, however, is a special place and holds a special place in her heart.

Now, I am not here to say one way or another about Betsy being clairvoyant, but she was certainly willing to teach me the ins and outs of the mansion and the spirits reported there. She is a true showman and holds an audience in the palm of her hand. Plus, she lets you experience some things that are not only strange and raise questions, but ones you should really experience yourself.

We check in just before four pm. There are others spending the night that night, but we essentially have the place to ourselves. The Lemp is a large dwelling that goes up three floors, back nearly to the highway—and then there is the basement. The whole grounds used to be even bigger and included huge limestone caves that had pools and a theater and a ball room. Much of that is gone now.

The mansion is nearly 200 years old. Right away, as soon as you get into the place, after climbing the steps and gazing at the white front and the many, many windows that look out onto the streets, highway, and parking lot like vacant eyes, there is a major creep-out factor.

I stay in the very large, very beautiful William Lemp Suite. This is named after William Lemp Sr., a man who helped the company grow to nearly epic proportions before shooting himself in the head in the very room where I slept after the tragic death of his son, Frederick. His wife, Julia, died of cancer in what is now the parlor of this room.

Across the hall is the Lavender Suite. This is a large suite complete with a bathroom and is named after Lillian Lemp, the wife of William Lemp, Jr. She had a penchant for wearing lavender and was known as "The Lavender Lady."

Down the hall is the Charles Lemp Suite. This is a smaller room but very nice. The bathroom is across the hall. Charles was the last Lemp to own the house and he first shot his beloved dog, Serva, before shooting himself in the head—possibly in that room or in the area that now serves as the bar downstairs.

Up in the attic, there used to be one bedroom and nothing else. It is the attic that supposedly is the most haunted. They have done some remodeling, however. Now there are three rooms, including the Elsa Lemp Suite. The Elsa Lemp suite is reportedly the most haunted suite in the entire inn. This is where my friends Scott and Jessica spent the night. The views are spectacular. All of the rooms in the attic are smaller, but very nice, and each has its own bathroom.

We spend a while looking around. It was still sunny. So, while things were eerie, the true creepiness did not descend until the sun did. I notice in my room a portrait of a barefoot peasant girl on the wall. The eyes of this painting are the scariest thing I have seen yet. The eyes are intense and, yes, follow me all around the room. We take a few pictures of that.

The Lemp is cluttered, littered, and bursting with mirrors. There are mirrors everywhere. There are mirrors on walls set up across from other mirrors. I don't know if this is some kind of effect the owners were going for or not. I just know that if you don't like your own reflection, or perhaps you are a vampire, the Lemp Mansion may not be for you.

We go out to dinner. We then go back to the inn. We settle in the William Lemp Suite. My friend's spouse talks about how she wants people to go on "missions." This was something that my two married friends have done the last time they had stayed at the mansion. Yes, my friends have been here before. In fact, this time around, is their third trip to the mansion. If there are ghosts, by this point, they know my friends by name.

The mission game calls for someone to be sent to some part of the house, such as the basement, and they are told to retrieve something from the location that would prove that they had been there. When the item was brought back, it would then be up to the next person to return the object to where it had been found. Her son agrees to be the first person to undertake a mission. His mission is to go down into the basement and retrieve a centerpiece from one of the tables down there. So, as the sun set, the boy set about his task....

The boy heads down the stairs. It is a rather tall mansion, so this took some time. The basement which had before been so well-lit and bright was now dark and gloomy. He said he looked down into the dark and had the following thought: *OH, GIVE ME A BREAK.* Still, his mother had dared him, so down he goes. He makes it into the basement and, at that point, hears something that sounds like someone dropping a fork or a spoon or some piece of silverware. That's about enough adventure for the young man. He grabs a vase with flowers from the center of the nearest table and runs.

He makes it back into the room panting and tells the story of the trip downstairs. He tells of finding the blackness. He tells of hearing the noise. Then he tells of running up the stairs. He holds a vase with flowers in his hand and he pants.

"Now it's your turn to bring it back," his mom says and she points at me.

I'd love to tell you I was so brave that I snatched that vase and flowers right up and ran back down there and then took the time to carefully place the vase and the flowers right back on the nearest centerpiece-less table. I'd love to tell you that, but it would be a lie. I completely and utterly chickened out. I laid an egg. I shed feathers. *BAWK!* The husband brings the vase back and he does it without so much as a second thought. (Author Note: Every ghost hunter suggests that if you go ghost hunting, you should never go alone. Whether you believe in ghosts or not, haunted mansions are dark and potentially risky places to crawl around in. While playing this game might be fun, you may want to try playing it in teams and with partners, just to be safe.)

We go downstairs for the ghost tour. We meet in the parlor which is just inside the main doors and on the right. Across from the parlor is what used to be the brewery office and this is where Billy Lemp, the Junior of the William's, decided he had had enough and shot himself in the chest at his desk. You can eat lunch and dinner there now.

Betsy has set up some pictures near one end of the room. We each pay our $15 and walk in and sit down. There are the others who will be spending the night, and then still others who have called Betsy about the every-Monday tours who ask if they could come along. She has told some of those folks to bring flashlights. People begin to gather and sit around tables. Some look nervous. Some look excited.

Betsy is not a particularly tall woman. She has brownish-red hair. She is wearing a white blouse and dark pants. She has a voice that carries easily. She introduces herself. Her daughter, it turns out, is the thin girl with dark hair who takes your money. She is also the one who holds up some of the pictures that Betsy talks about, holding them in front of her face and head while Betsy points.

Betsy tells the history of the Lemp Mansion, relating the tale of tale of a family that reached the heights of wealth and power in St. Louis, turning the history of brewing beer and how people celebrated after work on its ear—and then lost it all. She points out the map that shows how the underground limestone tunnels looked.

Then she says she is going to talk to some spirits. Holding up two L-shaped copper rods—she calls them "dowsing rods"—she explains that this is the same kind of thing that people have claimed can find water beneath the ground. She says that they are also used by ghost hunters. It seems that you can ask *yes and no* questions with them. As she talks, she holds them lightly in both fists and in front of her, and they slowly cross across her throat. She asks that they please be moved back somewhere else and they move back.

"Which way will be *yes*?" she asks. The rods move slowly to her left, our right.

"Thank you," she says. "Now, which way will be *no*?" The rods move slowly to her right, our left.

"Is this Billy Lemp?" she asks. The rods move slowly toward *YES*.

"Are you happy, Billy?" she asks. The rods move slowly toward *NO*.

"Are you upset with me?" she asks. The rods move slowly toward *NO*.

"Are you upset with one of my guests?" she asks. The rods move slowly toward *YES*.

I look over at the boy's mom. She is smiling at me and she points to me. Her son laughs at me. Just five minutes before, I had been standing at the top of the stairs looking at a portrait of a woman—a woman with dark hair and wearing black lace. She is not a very attractive woman. I made a disparaging comment about her. I have now come to find out that this was a portrait of Billy's second wife. The young boy's mom thinks this may have ticked Billy off.

I have to wonder. Betsy holds up more pictures. She tells how several members of the Lemp family killed themselves and how a few of them did it in this very house. She talks about how there are other spirits beyond the Lemps and about the spirit of a young girl named Sarah who lived in the place during its stint as a boarding house. She claims the girl was murdered and the murder was witnessed by the ghost of Charles Lemp. She states there is another ghost that was a caretaker of the place before it became such a tourist attraction who also wanders the halls.

Betsy's presentation lasts about an hour. Then it's time to walk the mansion. We stand and all of us cram into the area that had been the office, standing around the tables and lining the walls. She points out the portrait on the wall of "the Lavender Lady," and tells us about Billy.

As noted in the prior history of the mansion, Billy was slated to be the heir to the throne, but his father decided he liked his younger brother better. Then his younger brother died suddenly and his father shot himself. Suddenly, Billy was in charge. Billy, however, was a man with problems. He was cruel. He had animal fights in the limestone caves. He carried a gun. He was likely to flaunt the gun to anyone about and even intimidated his wife with it.

We move as a group into the area that is the bar. It's a small place. There are two lovely stained-glass windows on both sides of the bar. One is supposed to depict Lillian Lemp and the other, Billy Lemp. Neither looks remotely like either, judging from the photographs scattered about the place, however the stained glass work is lovely. The windows are not originals to the mansion. Betsy tells us that the large fish mounted above the bar, however, is.

Lillian Lemp was a very lovely woman—very tiny and just over four feet tall. She fought her husband Billy for custody of their son, William III and nearly lost custody when a photograph surfaced showing her smoking. These were the times Lillian lived in. However, the very large fish above the bar was caught by Lillian on a trip to Florida. She presented it to her father-in-law.

Betsy tells us that this room was once the Lemp library and then related the tale of Charles Lemp. The last Lemp to possess the mansion, he lived in the place almost entirely alone and had descended slowly into a kind of insanity. He became a germ-a-phobe. Then, one day, when he decided he had had enough, he became the only Lemp to write a suicide note. He then shot his beloved dog, Serva, and then he shot himself. She says it happened in the library, because by the time he did the dark deed, he was too sick to climb up the stairs to his room. She tells us that Serva also walks the mansion and that whenever she is seen walking around, Charles is close at hand.

We explore more of the downstairs and head into a back room that appears to be painted like a jungle. This is often referred to as "The Jungle Room." In fact, this room began its life as an atrium for Billy Lemp's mother. She loved nature. She loved animals. Apparently, the roof of this room was once all glass and had more windows. However, when Billy remodeled the inn to include brewery offices, the glass roof was removed to put in a room upstairs, and two windows were removed to support the weight.

A man in the group kicks a table and scares everyone. It's a guy in a dark shirt. He is a problem throughout the tour. He seems to have been dragged here and pays little attention to Betsy. In short, he is a disruptive influence. These things happen on tours.

Betsy says that there are by all accounts many animal spirits here. In addition to the Doberman that Charles Lemp had, there is also a smaller yapping dog and several cats, too. She also points out that the floor and the tile in the room is original. It's in pretty good shape for being nearly 200 years old.

We head into the room next door. It is a large dining room. Tables line the room. As soon as we enter, the dim light that hangs from the ceiling begins to flash. It brightens and then darkens. It does it slowly and then more rapidly. Betsy swears this never happens in this room. My friend says when she and her husband first spent the night at the mansion, they experienced that phenomenon in all rooms of the house. Ghosts? Or ancient wiring in an old house?

Betsy tells us that some ghosts are just energy that is recorded by a place and then played back. She relates two examples of this that happen in this room. In one, an older man is seen sitting at one of the back tables. He is dressed in older clothes. Whenever someone approaches him, he disappears. She says that up towards the front of the room, a family of three is often seen. They just seem out of place. As soon as they are seen, they often disappear. The light flashes some more. These apparitions, she says, appear only during the day.

Now we head upstairs, walking through darkened hallways. There is ancient thick carpet on the floor and mirrors along the walls. The place smells like a 200-year-old house. We all cram into a small room with a bed and a wardrobe that also happens to have a television and DVD player added. I am betting the ghosts do not use these much. The room is lit, but very dimly. There are two doors in and out of the place.

This is Charles Lemp's room, now called the Charles Lemp Suite. A sign just outside the room says that this may be the room where Charles committed suicide. Of course, Betsy tells a different story. Perhaps she heard it from Charles. Anyway, she tells us that Charles likes to appear in full view and in person. Betsy related the story of a man and woman who were in this room, and the woman suddenly awoke after sensing something moving. To her surprise, she opened her eyes to find an older gentleman in a suit with his arms crossed staring down at her from the foot of the bed. Her husband slept through it.

Here is where Betsy relates the story of the couple who thought they had the mansion to themselves and partied a bit too loud… only to find themselves confronted by an angry Charles Lemp.

Betsy now pulls out a cassette. She has made a relatively recent appearance on a local radio show that likes to broadcast at least once a year from the Lemp. Recently, when she appeared, she was discussing one of the rooms upstairs—the room in the attic where a deformed child supposedly lived out his entire life.

She plays the tape and you hear Betsy talking to the radio host. She mentions this child. Legend says that this child was deformed and perhaps mentally retarded. Some have suggested he might have had Down's Syndrome. He reportedly would be spotted by local children peering out of the windows of his room. His face was such that he received the horrible nickname of "The Monkey-Faced Boy." Betsy says, in fact, this child's name was Zeke. On the tape she mentions to the host that she believes the name of the child to be Zeke. Just after she says the name, and just before the host starts to talk again, you hear another voice, guttural, almost a whisper—something that was not heard when the conversation was live, but only heard afterward. Betsy and the host were in Zeke's supposed bedroom at the time.

"I'm Zeke," the voice says.

Betsy plays the recording several times in the dimness of the room so that we could all hear it. It's very creepy. Suitably freaked out and chilled, we move on. The best is yet to come.

We step out of the Charles Lemp Suite and head into the suite where I am planning on spending the night. Just before we all went downstairs, I had run into Betsy outside this room. She asked if I was staying there. I replied in the affirmative and she asked that I turn out some of the lights I had turned on and dim the over head lights. She explains at one point that this is like looking at stars when you are in the city. You can usually see one, maybe two, stars when you are standing in the middle of town. However, you get a few miles out of town and you can see all kinds of things you normally couldn't see. I am still not entirely sure how ghosts relate to stars, but it sure sounded cool at the time.

Anyway, we step into the William Lemp Suite. She comments that the lighting is perfect. We end up standing in the area where I intend to sleep later. My friend comments that there is a message waiting for me on my cell phone. (Somehow this seems very out of place.) Betsy tells us the story of William, commenting on how William shot himself in the head in this room and how Billy arrived, trying to kick down the door. She then tells us that William's wife, Julie, Billy's mother, died of cancer in the room right next door, which is now the sitting room area.

Julia is apparently also a ghost who walks these floors. Betsy advises us about ghosts who appear to walk about, but are unaware of anything that is going on around them. They are just going about their business, unaware of the living or the other dead who might be hanging around. Julia wanders the house looking for her sons and apparently, for Zeke.

As you might imagine, the young man in our group does not take kindly to the idea of a woman wandering around looking for her son.

Now, at last, it's time to head upstairs. The attic is the area reputed to be the most haunted. The friends I am with spent the night in the Lemp Mansion the first time several years ago, but even on their more recent trip, the attic area was completely unfinished. Yes, there was one room, the Elsa Lemp Suite, but the rest of the attic was barren. It was beyond barren, actually and, in places, starting to fall down. This is not the case now.

The Elsa Lemp Suite is right at the top of the stairs. To the left is what would have been a kind of balcony at one point. It has a gorgeous view. There is no railing around the cement edge, however, and the doors that lead out there are locked. There is now an ice machine in the small room that leads up to those doors.

Just past the Elsa Lemp Suite is a short hallway. The floors are carpeted. At the end of the short hallway, there are two new rooms that were not there until recently. The walls are painted. There are no holes in the ceiling. There is a kind of sitting room between the two rooms at the end of the hall and two chairs. There is also a soda vending machine and a snack machine that appear to be empty.

It's very strange seeing both the ice machine and the vending machines. There is an odd mix of period pieces and modern-day equipment. There are televisions in each room and DVD players and VCRs. There are CD and radio players. All mixed within the furnishings of yesteryear.

We head for the room to the left. The young couple from the town near Springfield, Illinois is staying in this room. The young man has dark hair and a scruffy beard. The woman is very blonde, very slim, and very beautiful. They are both very affectionate. They hold hands a lot. They appear a tad nervous that the next part of the tour is going to happen in their room.

"We're going to have a dark room session now," Betsy explains.

The room is not very big. Apparently, at one time, this room was part of Zeke's play room.

Betsy does not want to go into the Elsa Lemp room, which is back down the hall. The Elsa Lemp Suite is where my two friends are staying. Even the plaque outside the room says it's reputedly the most haunted room in the house. It's disturbing to me that, here Betsy is, a ghost hunter, and she doesn't want to go into the most haunted room. She says that before that room was remodeled and a bathroom added, it was a closet—and she saw something in there. She saw something that scared her. I worry for my friends who will sleep there this night. We have a frightened ghost hunter.

We all crowd into the room. Two of my friends end up across from me, with the bed in between. The young man of our group is standing directly behind me. There is a woman to my left who also claims to be clairvoyant. The two who are staying in this room are not far from us either, to my left, however. We hover near the walls. There is a window over my left shoulder. There is bathroom behind me and the door is open, nearly hitting my back.

Betsy comes in and she is carrying a flashlight. Betsy insists that everyone step further into the room. She doesn't want anyone to stand in the doorway. Her white blouse hovers in the dimness like some kind of a moon. It is very bright. She sits on the bed.

She advises us to open our minds and to then look at things around us. She reminds us that spirits often appear as just orbs of energy. Orbs are often caught on film whenever there is a haunting. One school of thought is that this is ectoplasmic energy left behind by traveling spirits. Another school of thought says that these are motes of dust caught in the flash of a camera because many of these old houses have a lot of dust.

Betsy says that orbs often appear to the naked eye as flashes of light. She tells us that most of these energies are white or a soft color, but warns us that anyone who starts to freak or sees anything orange or red floating in the air, that that person should let her know. She will stop the session.

Warning us that she will be turning off the lights now, she asks everyone to sit still. She shuts off the flashlight. Her blouse is now a disembodied blouse-shaped moon floating in the darkness.

"Spirits of the house," she says, "come and visit us now."

And, to my surprise, they just might have done exactly that…

"There's someone at the door," Betsy says. "Does anyone else feel or see anything?"

"There's someone right behind me," the supposedly clairvoyant woman next to me says. "He's leaning right up against me."

"There are more coming into the room," Betsy says. "I see a man peeking into the doorway."

Betsy's daughter is out in the hallway but standing off to the side. Betsy asks if she is okay. Her daughter replies that she is. Someone else lets loose with a kind of scream, nothing piercing, nothing like you would see or hear in a horror movie, but indicating that they see something or someone in the doorway as well.

Suddenly, a woman starts to yell. She is so terrified, she is speaking loudly in Spanish. Betsy is able to determine that she is freaked because she is seeing a red light.

My friend who happens to be the mother of the young man standing behind me, says, "That's the clock radio next to the bed."

Everyone kind of laughs. I look over and see the red digital numbers glowing. Betsy apologizes, saying that since it was behind her she did not see it. She then points out the glowing green light near the ceiling and lets us know that this is the fire detector. Betsy then advises that she wants to turn around to see the man who is supposedly leaning against the clairvoyant woman behind me.

"Yes," she says, "he is taller than you, isn't he?"

"Yes," says the woman.

"He's older than you too, isn't he?" Betsy asks.

"Yes," says the woman.

"I don't recognize that person," Betsy says. "I'm not sure who that is."

Again there is some commotion. Betsy once again asks if her daughter is all right. The indication from her is that she is fine. Someone has again seen something at the door.

"Serva is here," Betsy says, referencing the dog that was once Charles Lemp's. "Can any of you see her? She's coming right up to me."

Someone indicates that they can see the dog. Betsy then agrees to stand up from her position on the bed. The faded moon of her blouse moves. Just as that happens I notice a funny thing. She fades out. It is as if a black shadow has passed in front of my eyes. The room itself seems to get darker.

"Betsy," says my friend from across the room. "There's something funny going on with the light. You're fading."

"I see it too," I say.

At times her blouse almost fades out entirely. I wonder if I am having trouble adjusting to the light or if my mind is playing tricks on me. As I study her blouse, the weird fading in and out, and the strange shifting of shadows, I suddenly get the impression that someone is standing in front of me. Everyone in the room is a kind of shape, barely perceptible. So, my first thought is someone from the group has moved in front of me. I think, perhaps, it is someone who was standing behind me and wants a better look, or someone near the door has moved away from their location because they are freaked out. I get this image in my head that it is someone about my height standing just off to my left but wearing a baseball cap or hat—and that this someone is facing away from me, looking at Betsy. I can't explain it better than that. It's a feeling—an impression. For a moment I think the young man, who is standing behind me, has moved in front of me, because he is wearing a baseball cap.

"Okay," Betsy says, "I am going to turn on the light now. Oh, hello, there's a man standing next to me. I didn't even see him. I thought maybe he was part of the group."

It is then I realize that what is in front of me is the bed. There isn't room for anyone to be standing in front of me. They would have to be kneeling on the bed. Betsy turns on the lights. The space in front of me is empty. At my knees is the bed. Betsy is standing in the middle of the room. Everyone else is still standing along the walls. Just before she turned on the lights, I thought I saw some very quick, tiny, flashes of white light, like sparks, above what would be the wardrobe. I look there now and see a pale man standing there with his arms crossed. He is very real. I wonder if his paleness could have caused the impression of white. I wonder if reflections of light from the window behind me reflected off the finish of the wardrobe are what I saw.

Everyone is talking. Betsy says that this is the end of the tour and anyone can visit any other open room. She says she will be going downstairs to the parlor. If people want to talk some more she will be there. People are nervous. People are laughing. I have goose bumps everywhere.

Some people stop by to visit my friend's room and check out the supposedly scary bathroom. My friends show pictures of one of their trips to the mansion when the attic was not so nice and someone apparently put fake blood on the walls so it appeared to be dripping down.

I decide to head downstairs. My friend asks where I am going and I say I want to try out the dowsing rods. He rolls his eyes. Surprisingly narrow-minded from a guy who once thought it was okay to experiment with drugs. Meanwhile, messing with something none of us believe will actually work gets an eye-roll. The night is far from over and there is a whole mansion at our disposal.

The bathroom in Elsa Lemp Suite.

If you have a desire to create your own dowsing rods, you can do so by making a quick trip down to your local hardware store. It's a simple copper rod. The part that sticks straight out is about fifteen inches long. The part that you hold and that curves down is about five inches long. You simply hold them at your sides and fold your hands very lightly around them. You have to tuck your thumb against your fingers, as if you are making a fist. Do not rest the thumb on the rods. You then bring your hands up, bending them at the elbows, holding them out in front of you. Again, hold them lightly. By squeezing your fists you will see the rods move. You then have to ask *yes or no* questions.

I am standing in the parlor where the ghost tour began. There are others from the tour there as well. I am just a little embarrassed. On the other hand, I am kind of dying to try them. I find a spot near the rear entrance to the room and I am sort of whispering my questions.

"Which way will be *yes*?" I ask.

I hold the rods lightly. I swear that I did not move myself or my hands. However, the rods start to move. They move to the right. They keep moving to the right. They move until the one in my right hand touches my arm.

"Which way will be *no*?" I ask.

Once again the rods move. They move until they are straight in front of me and then keep moving all the way to the left. Again, I don't think I am doing this. I am not certain, however. Could they work on small, micro-pulses from my muscles? Could I be moving them without realizing?

"Are you Billy Lemp?" I ask. The rods move over to the right. *YES.*

"Am I the one you were mad at earlier?" I ask. The rods, after having moved back to the center position, moves all the way to the right. *YES.*

"Was it because of what I said about your wife?" I ask. Again, the rods move back to center and then to the right. *YES.*

"Will you accept my apology?" I ask. I get another *YES*.

My friend stops by and watches. "You're doing that, aren't you?"

"I don't think so," I say.

"Come on," he says.

"No," I say, "I'm serious. I don't think I'm moving them. At least, I am not doing so consciously. I don't know. I'm getting the answers I wanted to get. I'm getting the answers I was hoping to get, so, I have a hard time believing I am not doing it in some way."

He nods. His spouse tries it and she can't get them to work. I now notice others from the group all standing around. There's a blonde girl who thinks she is talking to Billy Lemp.

I decide to check out another room. I move into the office area where Billy Lemp shot himself. This time the rods tell me I am talking to Charles Lemp. I guess Billy is still across the hall hitting on the blonde girl. Charles tells me it's okay if my friends and I stay in the inn that night, that he won't bother us and that it's okay if I write my book. I get a few more people staring at me. Again, I admit that these are all answers I was hoping or wanted to get so it's hard to say if this is real or all just me doing it.

A picture is taken of me at the point where I am supposedly talking to Billy Lemp and I am holding the rods out in front of me. Right on my chest, in the picture, is a white sphere. It's an orb. However, there is also a very bright reflection of the overhead lights in the mirror located behind me. Could a reflection back into the lens if a digital camera cause something like that? I'm not sure.

Eventually, most of the people who were just there for the tour disappear. Some of us who are spending the night end up in the bar and we start talking. Betsy stops by and she talks as well. She discusses the fact that she will do some private tours and conducts all kinds of ghost-hunts. Interestingly, she says that she does not charge for ghost hunts in people's houses because she says it is an honor just to be invited into someone's home.

The author conducting a dowsing rod experiment.
Notice the orb on author's upper body.

At one point, I talk to her about some of the discrepancies between the history that she has told and the one I have done research on. She tells me she got the story of Zeke being a Lemp brother as opposed to an illegitimate son from Billy himself. She admits that the story of the house and the family who owned it is almost as compelling as the ghost stories.

Eventually, everyone who is not spending the night leaves. There is one other couple staying in the suite across from the one I am in and they were apparently there the night before as well. They are seen only briefly and they do not come downstairs with the rest of us. My friend has brought down a bottle of delicious red wine and a bottle of whiskey. The four of us sit in the parlor. We are soon joined by two other couples.

There is the older couple who is from Milwaukee. The husband of this group has his own bottle of whiskey. The second couple is the younger couple from a town in Illinois. She is the pretty blonde.

The lights dim and then grow brighter as we talk. Someone hears something near the back of the room. We tell stories that we have heard about the place. We learn about each other. I drink the great wine.

We spend hours together. We make a trip down to the basement and find it lighted and meet some guy named George who is the chef for the place. We sit in the atrium for a while and watch the lights flicker.

We have a good time. We talk about ourselves. We make sure the lights are dim. It's a tremendous amount of fun. We are in this together. We are scaring each other and making each other laugh. It gets late.

The rest of the group is tired. Despite the frightening moments in their room, the young man with the blonde woman heads off to their room. The couple from Milwaukee is right next door. Myself and my friends retire to their room for a while. The Elsa Lemp Suite is very nice, cozy, mostly wood and has terrific views. I see only one thing and that is a quick shadow that seems to dash past the open door of the room. I get the impression it is something on four legs, perhaps a dog. Then my friend closes the door.

We hear other things, mostly chimes, brief noises. We look at pictures on the digital camera and see more orbs in some of the pictures. Disturbingly, most of them are on me or covering my chest.

We spend some more time down in the William Lemp Suite. Eventually, my friend and his wife retire to their room. The young man and I share our room. We turn on every light in the place. It is fast closing in on two in the morning and I have a long drive the next day. I turn on the television and we sleep with the TV on.

The next morning, there is a prepared breakfast. We have a meal with the other couples, save for the ones who never came out of their room. What is terrifying, though, is the substance that the waitress insists is orange juice looks disturbingly like coffee with cream and sugar added. I am not sure if haunted oranges turn brown, but evidently haunted orange juice does. (The waitress even took sips of it in front of us as if to assure us it was safe!)

Eventually, we leave. In the days since I must say my affection for the place has grown. I cannot, even remotely, convey to you how much I think you should visit the Lemp Mansion. If you have any plans to go to St. Louis, you have to stop at this place! It is a restaurant during the day and they serve lunch and dinner. They have prime rib specials for lunch. There is a mystery dinner theater that performs there regularly as well. Every member of the staff has at least one story of something spooky happening to them. Whether it is slamming doors, whispered names, keys that fly out of their hands, or mysterious people who disappear, they all have a tale.

If you drive to St. Louis you will find the Lemp on the south side of the city. It isn't far from downtown being right across I-55 from the Anheuser-Busch factory. You will see a mural painted on the side of the mansion that shows a man pouring beer. Their motto is "Famous from Ghost to Ghost."

It is a bed and breakfast, but if you can afford it, stay the night. I mention it is a bed and breakfast because that means it is more expensive than the Holiday Inn down the road. The rooms are beautiful. Once the staff leaves, you have the place to yourself. It is even possible you could have the entire place to just you and your significant other.

The Lemp Mansion is located at 3322 DeMenil Place. Their phone number is 314-664-8024. If you can manage it, I suggest you spend the night there on a Monday night. It is worth the extra fifteen dollars to take the ghost tour with Betsy.

Betsy is a paranormal investigator and a lecturer. She conducts something called the St. Louis Spirit Search. They have a website at www.Stlspiritsearch.com and their phone number is 314-776-4667. She is a very nice woman with great stories that she loves to tell.

Since my stay, I can't stop thinking about my visit there. I would love to tell you I slept well that night in the big comfy bed. I cannot say that. I found the blankets a little warm and, I confess, I had them pulled up right over my head. I slept a bit, but it was not the most sound sleep I have ever experienced.

The beds are comfortable. The people I spent time there with were fantastic. The house is strangely beautiful and yet also undeniably spooky. The history is so thick, you can smell it.

Do I honestly think I saw ghosts? Do I honestly think I spoke to Billy and Charles Lemp with rods made out of copper? I don't know. I still don't think I have any better idea of whether or not ghosts actually exist. I just know that it was a lot more fun to think that it was possible. I think the world is a little more fun and interesting with the idea that ghosts are possible.

So, the next time you make a trip to Missouri or if you have plans to visit the Midwest, make a stop in St. Louis. There are a lot of great things to do there. However, if you have an interest in ghosts or the paranormal, then this is the place for you. Remember, back in 1981, *Life* magazine even declared the Lemp Mansion one of the top five most haunted places in the country and the Travel Channel recently put the mansion at number two. Call in plenty of time. If you try to get a room around Halloween, I say good luck. The place is booked solid then. They have a Halloween party in the place, though. They also host a New Years Eve party.

Just remember, you can change your reservations but you cannot cancel them. Yes, you can check out any time you like, but you can never leave.

Well, not really, but it's more fun to think so.

Part Four:
The Haunted Suburbs

Webster Groves is a suburb just west of downtown St. Louis—a beautiful suburb, but typical in many respects. Houses line street after street. Lawns shine brightly in the afternoon sun and are green and crisply mowed. Stores dot the corner with the big names on them and shops line the streets of Webster Groves. There are nice restaurants in downtown Webster Groves as well.

The international university known as Webster University is located and headquartered in Webster Groves. The original buildings that were once dormitories are still there. The newer buildings and student houses are also located in there. It's a peaceful place—a nice place, really.

There is another side to Webster Groves, however. There is the haunted side. There are ghosts lying behind the manicured lawns and the neat houses with their large porches. Hidden amongst those houses and those lives are restless spirits who like to walk when others sleep. At least three famous stories of ghosts walking the hallways of places located here come from Webster Groves.

The haunted suburbs.

Chapter Fifteen:
The Gehm House

A man by the name of Bart Adams originally built the house that still stands on Plant Avenue in Webster Groves. He built it in 1890, when there was little out that way except for countryside. He built it as a getaway, a country home, where he could spend time away from the big city and get away from it all. However, nothing much exciting ever happened with that house when Mr. Adams owned the property. No, the resident most people still remember, and still talk about, is a gentleman by the name of Henry Gehm.

Henry Gehm was a relatively wealthy man. He made his money in the railroad business by running a company that designed and built railroad cars. He was fond of leasing these cars to the traveling circuses of the time which has led to the legend that he was involved with the circus. This is not true, but he did have some small attachment to them.

Henry lived in the house on Plant Avenue from 1906 to 1944. It was believed that he died in the house, but subsequent research shows this is not the case. Henry Gehm died from cancer in his spine, in agony, in a hospital in 1944. However, it seems as though Henry never really left his house on Plant Avenue.

Henry was a stingy man. He preferred to both pay people and keep his money in gold coins. He did not trust banks. No, Henry preferred to hide his money and valuables all around his home and he built places to hide them. His house has become known as the house with "buried treasures."

It seems that the tales of ghostly activity in the house started around 1956, when a family by the name of Furry purchased the home. It was the wife, Fannie, who apparently first noticed that the house had something extra. It started simply, if a little strangely and creepily, when she began to be shaken awake by unseen hands every night at exactly two in the morning.

Fannie also reported that, one morning, she was awakened by what was clearly the sound of someone or some*thing* hammering on the headboard of the bed she was sleeping in. It was so loud it awoke her in terror, and she was certain that the headboard would be in splinters as though someone had taken a sledgehammer to it. When Fannie managed to get her wits about her and turn on the light, she found herself alone in the bedroom and the headboard still very much intact. Other times, Fannie reported that someone would beat against the windows in the middle of the night, and she could find no earthly explanation for it.

Things in the house began to move around. One morning, Fannie came downstairs to find a very heavy light sconce that had been bolted to the wall now lying on the floor. She also reported hearing footsteps at various times throughout the day and night. Always these footsteps marched from room to room and up and down the stairs as if someone were frantically looking for something. Always the footsteps ended at the top of the upstairs landing.

Fannie and her family managed to forget and even live with the sounds for many years. Fannie even grew accustomed to the strange sounds, passing them off as fancies of her imagination. The Furry family had poured a lot of their hard-earned money into this house. They had worked hard to make it what it was and they didn't want to leave it without a good reason. Ghostly sounds that could easily have been nothing more than imagination were just not good enough reasons.

It was the Furry's three-year-old daughter who woke them up to the fact that maybe something more was at work there than mere imagination. Children are often the ones in ghost stories who seem to be able to see things others can't. Many times in a ghost story, it is a child who sees the figure standing in the doorway or has the conversation with the person or persons that no one else can see. One morning, Fannie's three-year-old asked her mother who the woman in black was who kept coming into her room at night.

Reportedly, Fannie was quite stunned and curious about this question. She wondered aloud what her daughter was talking about. Her daughter said that there was an old lady dressed in black and often holding the hand of a young boy who liked to stop by her room at night. She also stated that this old woman in black would try to hit her with a broom, but that the broom did not hurt when it hit.

Once these reports began to surface, then Fannie and the rest of her family knew that it wasn't just their imaginations. They didn't like the idea that their daughter might be visited by strange women in the middle of the night. So, after nine years of owning the home, the Furrys put the home up for sale and moved out.

The next people to reside on Plant Avenue were the Walsh's. They rented the home in November of 1965. The people who rented the home to them did not tell the Walsh's that there were stories of the house being haunted. At first the family found nothing out of the ordinary.

One night, Clare Walsh was in her kitchen preparing dinner when she noticed the family dog was acting a little strangely. The dog was shaking in fear and cowering in a corner as though something were threatening it. When Clare looked in the direction of where the dog was staring, she saw an image standing in the kitchen doorway. It was a hazy, smoky shape roughly in the shape of a man. As Clare watched, the shape moved, hovering, gliding into the living room as a kind of shimmering mass and then vanished.

While this might certainly be a kind of wake up call to some, the Walsh's were not the kind to spook easily. Clare was suitably concerned and frightened, but she also soon forgot about the incident. Life resumed to normal for the Walsh's—for a while, anyway.

Before long, Clare and other members of her family began to notice the sound of footsteps wandering up and down the hallways and up and down the stairs. Eventually, Clare decided she had to find out the history of this house. She decided to ask a neighbor and found that her neighbors had once had an interest in buying the house, but had been told by another neighbor across the street that the place was haunted. Clare admitted to these neighbors that she was hearing ghostly footsteps at night.

The neighbors seemed to understand this. The neighbor from across the street helped confirm some of Clare's suspicions about the house, as well. The man across the street had been a guest in the house many times and said he knew that a man who once lived in the house had hidden valuables all over the property.

Was it possible that Henry Gehm still wandered the house looking for his lost treasure? Clare was not done with her checking. She noticed that the door to the attic refused to stay closed. Even when the door was latched, she would find the door standing open. She checked the step beneath the attic door and discovered that the tread on that step lifted off to reveal a hiding spot beneath. Clare also realized that when the footsteps would be heard on the stairs, this last step was often where the steps would stop.

She began to notice the attic door. Once when her husband and she were spending the night in different rooms due to an illness, Clare lay awake and listened to the attic door. As she did so, the door opened and then closed at least four times.

Another morning, Clare paused to once again shut the attic door and then went downstairs. Sometime during that morning she had the urge to check the attic door again and she made her way up. She found the door standing open, and when she went inside, she found everything that had been neatly stacked in the attic room was moved. A chest of drawers that had been standing against one wall had not only moved, but one of the drawers was now hanging open. As she approached, she noticed that the drawers were full of blueprints, and when she studied them closely, she saw that the name on the blueprints was "Henry Gehm."

Still the house remained unsettled. The endless marching at all hours continued. One morning, Clare found all of the drawers in a piece of furniture in her dining room had been rearranged. Clare also found the clothing in one of here dressers scattered about.

The Walsh's became convinced that there were two spirits in the house. One was the old man who liked to walk all over the house and up and down the stairs. The second, they came to believe, was that of a child. They did not report ever seeing a woman in black—with or without a broom.

Strange events continued. Now there were voices and cries in the middle of the night. A typewriter in one room sprang to life on its own and began typing. The attic door continued to open and close on its own. The Walsh's dog became a frightened beast, walking with its tail down and whimpering. Eventually, it was enough for the Walsh's. They had a brand new house build elsewhere and moved out.

Today, a family known as Wheeler owns the house on Plant Avenue. They bought the home and changed it from a rental property into a home where they could live and raise their children. Despite their seemingly idyllic life, the Wheelers do believe that their house in haunted.

The Wheelers state that, much like the Walsh's, their dog acts strangely and will stand and stare at empty places with a deep growl in its throat and a tail pointed straight. The Wheeler's son also complained of being awakened in the middle of the night due to someone or some*thing* shaking his bed. They have also seen shapes moving about the house, found things moved, heard ghostly footsteps, and things moving in the attic.

Unlike the Lemp Mansion, however, the Gehm House is a private residence. The current residents say they still will get people who like to stop by and want to hunt for buried treasure. Mostly, the residents want to continue to reside in the home and be left alone. Their house may be famous, but they prefer a life of relative anonymity.

Some research has indicated that Henry Gehm may have lost a young grandson during the time he was in the house. No one knows who the reported woman in black was. No one can be sure the male spirit is that of Henry Gehm, perhaps constantly looking for his hidden coins and treasure.

(Author note: This is an actual residence, not a bed and breakfast. The house is not publicized. Respect is required for any ghost research activities.)

Chapter Sixteen:
The Ghost Girls

Also located in Webster Groves is a building that seems to have a very humanitarian purpose. It is a treatment center for children who are victims of abuse or who have been abandoned. What this does not tell you is that the house has a history going back into the 1800s, and of the mysterious apparitions and spectacles that have been associated with the property.

Known as the Rock House, it is actually listed as a National Historic Landmark. The house sits on twenty-three acres these days and provides care to the children who need help. However, the home began life in another part of the city and was known as St. Louis Protestant Orphan's Asylum. It was initially started to house orphans from the cholera epidemic in 1832.

The needs of the home began to expand after the Civil War. The home merged with the Western Sanitary Commission and moved to the Rock House location in Webster Groves. The home now also provided relief for veterans of the Civil War in addition to the services for orphans.

The Rock House was an interesting choice because it already had an interesting history. The house was built in 1850 by a man named Reverend Artemus Bullard. Bullard operated the home as a seminary until he died in a train wreck in 1855. Bullard was a staunch abolitionist and many believed that the Rock House was a station on the Underground Railroad.

There is evidence to support this theory. There was a tunnel beneath the Rock House than ran for several blocks. It is believed this was a hiding spot for runaway slaves. Eventually, the entrance to this tunnel was sealed off when, sometime in the 1890s, two children died when they became lost in the tunnels.

Just to add to the mystery of the place, the Rock House was gutted by fire in 1910. The entire home was nearly completely destroyed. Along with the destruction of the home, one of the children died in the fire. The fire wrecked the interior of the home, but the stone walls that made up the outside remained tall and strong. The home was rebuilt.

In 1944, the home changed its name and altered its purpose. It became the Edgewood Children's Center. The home also changed from taking care of orphans to helping emotionally disturbed children.

Over the years, there have been hundreds of children who have lived within the walls of the Rock House. Unfortunately, given the nature of the work that was done there and considering it was the residence of many children, there were also many deaths of children. Given the long history of the place and the fact that there have been some mysterious deaths on and around the property, the rumors of the property being haunted have continued.

One of the most often reported spirits has been the ghostly image of the little girl who supposedly died in the fire back in 1910. The little girl is said to be very friendly, and the current staff of the Rock House have even given her the name Rachel. Some have reported that they see a little girl standing under a tree on the property. This isn't so strange until you consider that most of the reports say this little girl is floating.

There are reports of footsteps that run up a stairway that no longer exists but did a long time ago in a previous century. People who have spent time living on the second floor say they have seen objects moving on their own and have heard other phantom footsteps. Others have reported the feeling of being watched or a nearly overwhelming feeling of uneasiness.

The tree on the grounds seems to be a center for activity. Others have reported the sounds of children playing beneath the tree when the area beneath was empty.

The Rock House continues to this day. It is located at 330 North Gore Street right near the downtown Webster Groves area. It is a not a place where you can take a tour, like the Lemp Mansion, but you can drive by it. Perhaps, just perhaps, if you slow down and the children feel like playing, you might see a little girl or hear the sound of children playing beneath a cottonwood tree.

Chapter Seventeen:
The University

Time now for another personal tale of hauntings. While this is not one generally found on various ghost-hunter sites or anything of that nature, there is a personal experience I have had at a place rumored to be haunted and located in Webster Groves. Up until my night at the Lemp Mansion, my only experience with something I couldn't explain occurred at this place.

There is a university that takes up a lot of space in Webster Groves. It covers several blocks. These days, the bookstore is even located downtown. The signature building of Webster University is the original main campus which is located on Lockwood Avenue. The building has old architecture, different from the modern buildings that dot the campus. The administrative building is old with stone turrets that reach majestically into the sky. Before the entire building was recently converted into offices, the aged building was also a dormitory.

This is where I spent my college years. Back then, there were two dormitories. When you were a freshman, you got to stay in the newer dorms called Maria Hall. Every year after that, if you wanted to continue to live on campus, you moved into the older section which was known as Loretto Hall.

The part of the university known as Loretto Hall has a long history, like so much in St. Louis. The building is old with creaky wooden floors and ancient creaky plumbing. It's the kind of place that constantly attracts dust. Some rooms have only a sink in a closet with a communal shower and bathroom down the hall.

Some other rooms share a bathroom with an old bathtub and no shower, leaving the residents to install their own shower heads. The rooms are not very big and have wooden floors. The doors are wooden with smoked glass near the tops of them. There are only a few outlets given the ancient electrical system in the building. This leaves long snaking trails of electrical cords extending across floors, under beds or hidden beneath carpets.

The Loretto Hall was once a convent. In years past, the cloistered life of a nun was the perfect one for the small rooms with few modern conveniences. When you stand in the creaky hallways or walk up the creaky stairs you can almost imagine the nuns padding this way and that, silently from room to room.

Near the far end of each hall are the turrets. These are semi-circular rooms that overlook the parking lots and the grounds that face out to the north. Each turret has large wood-framed windows that can be opened to let in a breeze. The windows are without screens making for interesting sitting arrangements at times. It is in one of these turrets where the legends begin.

There seems to be something about old stone buildings that is conducive to ghost stories. Whether there are true legends or not, it seems if you have an old stone building, you are likely to also have ghost stories surrounding that building. This appears to be the case with the Loretto Hall of Webster University.

The legend of the wandering nun was there almost from the first day I arrived. It was pretty much a part of the orientation. The legend says that back in the day when it was a convent, there was a young nun housed there. She apparently fell in love with a man. The rumors of who this man was vary. Regardless of who he was, they entered into a relationship that ended with the nun being pregnant. Disgraced and despondent, the rumor was that this nun made it to the fourth floor turret and threw herself out the window to the concrete below.

The legends of the wandering nun were handed down from one class to the next. The stories were that she would sometimes be seen in the fourth floor turret as a kind of apparition and that she would disappear when approached.

Others reported that sinks would turn on in bathrooms or that lights would turn on and off as though by ghostly hands. Others reported hearing voices or footsteps that were attached to nothing—or no one anyone could see.

Of course, the university denies that there are ghosts. There was even a story run in the school newspaper about the "ghost nun." The legend was disputed and it was stated that no record of a nun ever committing suicide on the property existed. Still the rumors persisted and probably do to this day.

As for me, the only strange experience I ever had in the dorms, oddly enough, was not in the older Loretto Hall but in the Maria Hall when I was a freshman. In this dorm, each room shared a bathroom with a neighbor neighboring room creating a suite. Thus, you had a roommate and suite-mates. My room, during the first part of the year, was on the third floor of Maria Hall.

One night, myself and my roommate were sitting in my room. In the room next door, our suite-mates were also sitting. All of us were doing homework. Suddenly, without warning, the shower in the bathroom that connected both rooms turned on. I looked at my roommate. He looked at me. We had always had trouble with the shower in that room. We stood and walked into the bathroom. To our surprise, both of our suite-mates were also standing there. None of us were in the shower and yet the water was running at full blast.

We made jokes and someone turned off the water. The rumors of the ghost nun came to our minds and we made more jokes. Still, none of us could explain how a shower could turn on full blast all by itself.

The other rumors of spirits on the university campus can once again be found in the older part of the administrative building. In the older Loretto section of the building is an area known as the Loretto-Hilton Center. This is a kind of assembly hall with a stage near the front. There is also a screen that drops down and films are shown.

A new rumor, at least to me, is that someone once died in that auditorium and now prowls the Loretto-Hilton Center. One story says a technician was working upstairs, perhaps on the film projector equipment, and found himself nearly falling off of the upper balcony into the seats below. A ghostly hand grabbed him and prevented him from falling.

These days, the Loretto Hall is no longer a dorm. New housing was built that more approximates apartments for the students to live in. I am not even sure if Maria Hall is used for housing any longer. The Loretto Hall was turned into offices and class rooms. Whether or not workers in the building still see the ghostly nun prowling the halls and pining for her lover is unknown.

Interestingly, one of the things that Webster University does is buy up the houses in the area. These homes are turned into classrooms and offices. Many of these houses are donated by former owners. Most of them are old. Despite this there are no other rumors of ghosts in those houses, but I am sure it all depends on who you speak to.

Part Five:
The Civil War

The Civil War was, of course, a great tragedy for the entire country. However, the state of Missouri experienced parts of the Civil War that no other parts saw. Located in a strange kind of limbo between north and south, Missouri had strange kind of neutral stance when it came to the issue of slavery. However, internally many in the state were divided.

Missouri became a kind of no-man's land during the last days of the war. Aspects of guerilla warfare were practiced by Confederate soldiers who staged regular raids on any and all who lived within the Missouri borders. Brutal acts were committed against soldiers and residents, the likes of which would not be heard again until Vietnam.

Most of St. Louis was free from this warfare. St. Louis, in fact, became a kind of outpost for the northern army. Many areas were used by the northern army for ammunition and prisons for Confederate soldiers.

St. Louis had plenty of southern sympathizers. Some of them left the city and the state when the war started and never returned. Others did and some of them became very interesting characters.

Of course, some areas of St. Louis that were used for various purposes during the war grew legends. Many of them were horrific legends and legends of ghosts. Restless spirits were everywhere in St. Louis when the war ended.

Chapter Eighteen:
The Medical School that Became a Prison

One of the more interesting characters to come out of St. Louis during the Civil War era was Dr. Joseph McDowell. The doctor established the first truly successful medical school west of the Mississippi. His McDowell Medical College was located at Ninth and Gratiot Street and became hugely successful.

Even as the school became a success, the strangeness of Dr. McDowell became legendary. He was talked about all over the city not for his teaching methods but for his behavior. He was described as being erratic and having an explosive temper. He was very jealous of other doctors and other schools. He was also a firm believer in slavery and a passionate secessionist. He was known to be generous and giving to the poor but he was also know to hate Catholics and immigrants—and especially blacks. McDowell would often be spotted standing on street corners near his residence preaching at length about these subjects. He was also known to wear a breastplate from a suit of armor beneath his clothes because he believed his enemies would try to kill him.

The school McDowell built was constructed to his very exacting specifications and had some very unique attributes for a place of learning. The school was designed with two huge Greek Revival wings which were flanked by an octagonal tower. The tower was fitted with a deck that contained six cannons. McDowell claimed these cannons were to protect the school against any form of attack. McDowell also stocked the school with muskets that he would hand out to students should the school be attacked.

The strange parts of the school did not end with the armaments. The central tower was also constructed with niches. These were large enough for bodies to be placed in. McDowell wanted to be able to place family in these niches upon their deaths. As if this wasn't strange enough, McDowell planned to place the members of his family in copper tubes which would then be filled with alcohol and then placed in a niche. The idea behind this was to preserve the bodies of his loved ones forever.

McDowell was a big believer that his students should be able to study anatomy. In addition, he was a huge believer that students should be able to study bodies as they were dissected. It would be this particular belief and practice that would gain the doctor notoriety. In those days, dissection was illegal in the United States. Finding bodies to dissect was very difficult. So, McDowell introduced his students to grave robbing.

The school was already considered a haunted place and generally avoided by the public before the Civil War even broke out. However, sometimes mobs, upon hearing where the doctor was getting his study materials, would attack the school. It was at this time that the cannons would roar and the muskets would be handed out. One story says that McDowell released a pet bear that was living in the basement of the school to successfully disperse an angry mob.

McDowell himself became an ardent believer in ghosts when an incident involving a mob and a stolen body nearly cost him his life at the hands of a lynch mob. The legend is that a young German girl in the neighborhood of the school died from a mysterious disease. McDowell and his students wanted to study that body. They snuck into the cemetery and dug up the body, then bringing it back to the school. When the family of the young girl found out about it, they went storming for McDowell.

McDowell received advanced word of the mob and got ahead of them. Entering the school, he made his way to the dissection room so he could grab the body and hide it. His plan was to hide the body in an attic, and he slung it over his shoulder and started the climb to the attic. As he was climbing, McDowell reported that he saw the ghost of his mother appear before him. She warned him to hurry and that intruders had already entered the school. McDowell quickly hid the body and then looked for a place to hide himself. His mother's ghost reportedly appeared to him again and told him to hide in the autopsy room. So, McDowell went into the room and hid himself under a sheet as the mob searched the school. (It was after this event that McDowell decided to place the bodies of his loved ones in copper tubes filled with alcohol to preserve them.)

McDowell purchased a limestone cave near Hannibal, Missouri. When his daughter died at the age of fourteen, he placed her in a copper tube. He filled that tube with alcohol and then placed that tube in the limestone cave. Despite adding a thick steel door to the room where he placed the tube, the locals around the cave pried open the door, removed the tube, and put it on display.

When McDowell's wife died, he purchased a mound near the Illinois town of Cahokia. He had a tomb built on top of the mound and his wife was placed inside it. Rumors said that McDowell would at times look at the tomb with his telescope from a spot on top of his home.

McDowell's son joined the Confederate Army when the Civil War broke out. His son took two of the cannons from his father's school with him when he left. McDowell also shipped off the muskets and other armaments he had stocked within the school to the southern army. McDowell himself abandoned the school and provided his services to the southern army as a doctor and surgeon.

The school was commandeered by the Federal Army and turned over to Major Butterworth. Butterworth, in December of 1861, took fifty men and started converting the medical school into a prison. They discovered wagonloads full of human remains including bones and body parts. They converted the rooms into cells and turned the doctor's beloved dissection room into a dining hall. A Colonel Tuttle was given charge of the prison.

Prisoners began to arrive on December 22nd of the same year. It wasn't long before it was evident how poorly the school would serve as a prison. In fact, the entire conversion had been rushed and poorly planned. The capacity of the entire building was about one third of the amount that arrived on that very first day. Not enough latrines and waste facilities had been constructed.

The treatment of prisoners was harsh at the Gratiot Street Prison. Guards were told to shoot prisoners who tried to escape and also prisoners who simply stuck a head or any part of their body out of a window. It was rumored that the tower guards would often take target practice at the prisoners inside by shooting through the windows.

As though the treatment by the guards was not enough, the inside of the place had become a kind of dungeon. Two large areas inside were converted into housing areas for prisoners. These rooms became known as the "round room" and the "square room." The round room was the smaller of the two rooms and was still described as dark and gloomy and filthy. This room was in the middle section of the octagonal tower. There were usually 250 men crammed into the space.

Even though things were cramped and filthy in the round room, it was a paradise compared to the square room. The square room was about seventy by fifteen feet and held another 250 men. However, this room had virtually no ventilation. Descriptions of this room say it was run without regard to any form of hygiene. As you might imagine disease ran rampant through this room and the rest of the prison.

Things started out badly and then got worse as the war went on. Hundreds of men were crammed into this building. Every nook and cranny was converted into space without regard to hygiene. Vermin ran over the bodies of the prisoners. The sound of men coughing and moaning could be heard for blocks. The food rations weren't enough to feed all of the prisoners and prisoners began dying at a rate of four a day.

When the war ended the prison was closed down. McDowell toured Europe for a while and then returned to St. Louis. He converted the prison back into a school. He remodeled the entire school except for one room which he left exactly as it was as a kind of reminder. He supposedly referred to that one room as "Hell" and put a rattlesnake, crocodile, statues of Satan and a gallows from which he hung an effigy of President Lincoln.

Eventually, the creepy Dr. McDowell died of pneumonia in 1868. The school closed down again and the building was left vacant and left to rot. The place was already feared, but now the abandoned building became the source of more ghost stories.

Stories began to filter out of the place. Residents around the former prison and school claimed they could see ghostly faces out of the windows. Clothing and movement would also be seen. Those brave enough to actually approach the building claimed they heard screaming and wails of pain from inside the building. The sounds of screams and grown men weeping could often be heard blocks from the actual building.

Rumors of ghosts in the building continued until the building itself was declared unsafe and a fire hazard. Even the octagonal tower was torn down in 1882. Today, nothing remains of the McDowell Medical College or the prison it became. The spot today is occupied by a parking lot for the Ralston Purina Company.

Chapter Nineteen:
The Barracks

The area of St. Louis known as the Jefferson Barracks was originally established as a fort in 1826. The place was named, as you
might have guessed, for President Jefferson who had died the same
year the fort was established. The first duties for the new fort was to
house soldiers and protect settlers in the area from Indian attack.

For a long time, the Jefferson Barracks were used as a kind of
staging area as well as a military hospital. There is a National Cemetery located on the establishment and that was created in 1863.
Tales of ghosts originate in the areas where old buildings used to
stand or where older buildings still stand and exist today.

Nearly every area of Jefferson Barracks has a ghost story. From
the area that was commissioned as a veteran's hospital to the cemetery, and all of the buildings in between, there are stories of strange
happenings and ghostly apparitions.

One of the stories most often repeated is of a Halloween party
being held in the hospital. Some officers who were working security
at the gate made a comment to one of the party organizers that one
of the guests had been wearing an amazingly authentic Civil War
officer uniform. The organizer was puzzled and commented that
none of the guests had been wearing such a costume. The officer was
equally as confused because he had distinctly remembered seeing a
man enter the hospital grounds wearing a Civil War officers uniform
and he had assumed it was someone coming to the costume party.

Whether or not this story has any basis in fact is disputed by the
fact that another version of the story also circulates. According to the
second version, the same party was going on and one of the party

officials noticed a man dressed in a Civil War uniform sitting on a stone wall just past the crowd. The host walked over to the man and asked him how he was enjoying the party. Reportedly, he received a rude reply that the party was fine. The host turned to walk away, and when he turned back, the man was gone. Later, the host asked one of the other guests where the man in the Civil War uniform had gone, only to find that no one else saw such a guest and such a costume at the party.

Other tales come from the Civil War era itself when soldiers stationed there guarded the train depot and the railroad tracks nearby. At least one story says that a guard approached a man walking down the hill from the railroad tracks only to realize as he approached that the man was "blurry" and indistinct and then vanished all-together.

Stories about the hauntings in the headquarters building abound even to this day. There are stories of footsteps walking up and down the hallway. There are other stories of people heard speaking and moving around in rooms that turn out to be empty.

One of the oldest ghost stories is a supposed ghost who still wanders around the area that at one time was the powder magazine. The building is a huge limestone building and was used to store rifles and gunpowder. The story goes that around World War II sentries used to have to guard the area around the ammunition site.

Sentries who were assigned to guard the ammunition depot reported seeing a soldier in old clothing who would show up and challenge the other sentries, demanding to know who they were. The worst part was that this ghostly sentry had a bullet hole in his head that ran with blood. Reportedly, one sentry who was confronted by this sight was so terrified, he left the army and never returned. The story is that this was a soldier killed years before when a raiding party attacked the ammunition depot.

Building 28 is a building that was still in use up until recently. The building was initially designed to be a barracks and house soldiers. It is still the home of the 218th Engineer Squadron.

Men working in the buildings report hearing footsteps in the hallways. One story says that a man who was working in the building late at night heard footsteps on the second floor directly above the room where the man was working. Thinking it was just someone else working late, the man kept working. Later when he wandered upstairs to see who else was there, he found the room above his closed and locked. He went back downstairs to continue working, and no sooner had he sat back down in his chair, when he heard footsteps again directly above his head. This time he decided it was best to call it a night and he left.

One of the more modern stories comes from the 1980s when several officers and some other non-commissioned officers were working late in the building. They decided to leave and turned off the lights. They all ended up in the parking lot only to look back at the building. To everyone's surprise a light was on in the office they had just left.

One of the officers sent one of the lower-ranked NCOs back into the building to turn off the light. The man did and walked back. Again, they looked back and saw the light was still on. Yet again, the lowly non-commissioned officer was sent back into the building to shut off the light. As the other men watched, the NCO entered the building, walked up the stairs, and into the office. They could see his shadow as he shut off the light. As he came back out into the parking lot they all looked up to see the light on again.

Since the building was old the officers figured the wiring was just bad. But the story didn't end there! Once again, this poor lowly officer was sent back into the building. They waited until he came back. This time they didn't bother to look up and just got into their cars and drove home.

The buildings are still there and they are still in use. The tales of ghosts continue to come and the ghostly footsteps still wander the halls of the older buildings.

Part Six:
The Illinois Side

The thing to remember about St. Louis is that the entire area really occupies two sides of the Mississippi River. There is the city of St. Louis itself which is located on the Missouri side of the river and then there is East St. Louis and all of the small towns and cities that line the Mississippi just a short drive or distance from downtown St. Louis on the Illinois side. There is a road that runs up the Illinois side, right along the river and passes through towns like Alton, Grafton and little Elsah. I recommend you take this drive if you ever get the chance to visit the St. Louis area.

There is a lot of Native American culture on the Illinois side. Just east of St. Louis is the town of Cahokia. At one time, it is believed a Native American city that was more densely populated than London existed here. There are tourists attractions here now, but there are also the famous Cahokia Mounds. Exactly what these mounds were used for is unclear but there are many bodies buried in the area and the mounds are rumored to have had great religious significance.

Not far from Elsah is the Piasa Bird. This is a legendary Native American story about a monstrous bird who terrorized the local citizens. A brave chief helped defeat the bird and the bird is now painted on the rocks that overlook the Mississippi River. You can see the Piasa Bird if you travel along the river.

The city of Alton is also located there. The strange thing about Alton is that it is usually mentioned when people list most-haunted cities in the country. It is a town rather famous for its antiques.

There is even a riverboat gambling casino located in Alton. Alton also has a claim to fame in that it was the home of the "Gentle Giant," a man who was once the tallest man in the world.

The Alton area is also famous for at least two very haunted buildings. They are old historic buildings just like many of the places in St. Louis. In many ways these buildings are even scarier than the other haunted buildings on the Missouri side.

Chapter Twenty:
The McPike Mansion

The most haunted place in Alton is a mansion that must have been hugely grandiose in its prime. Pictures of the place now take some imagination to see what must have been a gorgeous mansion in its day. It appears to be even larger than the Lemp Mansion, but over the years, vandals and nature have taken its toll on the McPike Mansion. Much of the home is unsafe now. Entire staircases are now just gone. Parts of the second floor are now collapsed.

The home was built in 1869 for a man with the rather unusual name of Henry Guest McPike. Mr. McPike was wealthy enough to afford one of the most famous architects of the time, Lucas Pfeiffenberger, to design the mansion. Pfeiffenberger had also designed other famous buildings around the area like the St. Mary's Church, Grace Methodist Church, and schools named after Presidents Lincoln and Garfield.

Henry Guest McPike ended up in Alton as a very young man when his father, John McPike, moved to the area from Kentucky. Before that, the McPike family was from Scotland. Henry and his family became very active members of Alton society. Henry himself started a number of businesses throughout his life and worked as a real estate agent, box manufacturer, and an insurance executive. He was also president of the oldest horticultural society in Illinois.

At the same time Henry was moving from one business to another, Pfeiffenberger was also becoming a staunch Alton citizen. He became active as a member of the Alton Volunteer Fire Department and even became Alton's mayor from 1871 through 1883.

Pfeiffenberger is also the one credited with getting Alton's streets paved and having curbs and gutters installed.

While Pfeiffenberger was active in politics, Henry Guest McPike seemed to be trying to avoid entering the political arena. Despite his father being active in the Whig party and expressing interest in the abolitionist movement, Henry didn't really seek political office even though the community offered political offices to him several times.

During the years of the Civil War, Henry was asked to fulfill the role of Deputy Provost Marshall of the District. This position put him in a management role in the War Department. Shortly after this, Henry acted as a political representative in political conventions and the city council. Alton then elected Henry mayor from 1887 to 1891.

Henry's mansion was built in a style referred to as Italianate-Victorian. Whatever the name, it was easily the most elaborate and beautiful home in Alton. The mansion is made up of sixteen rooms and a vaulted wine cellar. The home was built on what was then referred to as "Mt. Lookout" and the entire estate was planted with exotic trees, plants, and orchards. Henry even became famous for developing and growing the McPike grape which became known all over the country.

The history of the mansion itself is a tad muddled. Some say that the McPike Mansion stayed occupied by the McPike family until the 1930s. However, another story says that the mansion changed ownership to a man named Paul A. Laichinger in 1908, and that he lived there until he died in 1930. Some also say Paul Laichinger rented the home to others instead of living there himself.

What *is* known is that the mansion has been on the National Register of Historic Places. Sadly, these days it is also known to be on the list called the Landmarks Preservation Council of Illinois'—the list of the ten most endangered historic places in the entire state. Time has not been kind to this beautiful and historic mansion.

The mansion began to fall into disrepair in the 1950s. It was during this time that the home was finally abandoned by any residents and left empty. Almost immediately, vandals took a liking to the place. The home has been, essentially, looted for decades. Windows were broken. Beautiful fixtures in the homes were broken or stolen. The woodwork, once ornate and beautiful, has been decimated and nearly completely destroyed. The floors have deteriorated to the point where people cannot walk on them.

Thankfully, there is some hope. In 1994, a couple by the name of Luedke bought the home at an auction. They have been trying since then to raise the money needed to repair the mansion. The price tag is daunting, but they hope to turn the mansion into a tourist attraction or bed and breakfast.

Stories abound about spirits in the McPike house. As you might imagine, a gorgeous old mansion located just off the beaten path would automatically be labeled at haunted. Vandals have claimed to have seen and heard things within the walls of the mansion. It is also a favorite of psychics and ghost hunters, and they all have stories and theories of who or what haunts the grounds of the McPike mansion.

How many of these stories can be trusted or believed is open for debate. There is someone who has stories of ghosts in the house that has some credibility, and that's Sharyn Luedke, one of the owners. She claims that the spirit of Paul Laichinger, the second owner, still likes to walk around on his property.

Sharyn has reported that the first time she ran into one of the spirits was about six months after her and her husband bought the place. Sharyn had shown up to water some plants growing on the property. As she stood out on the lawn with her hose, she looked back at the house and saw a man standing in the window looking back at her, or perhaps out at the lawn. As she watched, the man slowly faded away. Sharyn was able to see him distinctly enough to report that he had been wearing a striped shirt and a tie. Sharyn has recently discovered an old photograph of Mr. Laichinger wearing the same shirt and tie.

Sharyn has also told other investigators, and those interested in the haunting of the McPike house, that she believes the ghost of a former servant named Sarah also still resides in the home. Sharyn had dubbed this spirit Sarah without really knowing the name, until a man stopped by the home one day and presented the Luedkes with some books that he had taken from the house many years before. When Sharyn looked through the books she found the name of Sarah Wells written inside one of them. Sharyn also reports being touched and even hugged by this spirit and that the spirit is often found on the third floor along with the scent of lilacs.

Over the years, the home has been the hangout of local teenagers. The home has been the place to dare friends to enter and perhaps take things from inside. The home as it has deteriorated has begun to look haunted, and thus continued to produce stories of ghosts. Apparitions and faces at the window seem to be the common theme.

One of the creepiest parts of the mansion is the vaulted wine cellar. The ceiling is very low to the ground, and the entire area is made of stone. Needless to say, it is also very dark. There is a heavy metal door that seals off one area. At least one investigator reports on his website that he was part of an investigation that was exploring this area. Someone in the group decided they needed to go upstairs because of the cramped quarters in the wine cellar. This female member of the group was escorted upstairs by another member who said she would return. As the group waited, they heard the steps go up and then heard steps coming back down. The heavy metal door swung open and the group was surprised to find no one there.

The McPike Mansion is still a favorite place for those who claim to hunt ghosts. Some try to camp out on the property and have parties there. It is, technically, private property now, although the Luedkes do allow tours from time to time. They are still trying to raise money to save this historic house. If you happen to be in Alton, you can stop by the Alton Visitor's Center for more information.

Chapter Twenty-One:
The Mineral Springs

Alton, Illinois, as mentioned prior, is known as a place to go and shop for antiques. The downtown area is filled with beautiful stores filled with them. One of those is located on Broadway right downtown. It is a kind of antiques mall with numerous antique stores—well known and shopped by anyone looking for antiques of all kinds. What is not generally known is that this location was once one of the most popular places in the entire St. Louis/Alton area. In fact, the building was once a hotel with supposedly healing waters running beneath it.

Two people who had nothing to do with the hotel business opened the Mineral Springs Hotel in 1914. August and Herman Luer were actually in the meatpacking business when they looked into the property as a place to store ice. Very successful businessmen in the meatpacking industry already, they started digging to build their ice storage building. As they were digging, much to everyone's surprise, a natural spring was discovered. A test from a local chemist declared that the waters had "medicinal" properties. It was the chemist who suggested to August and Herman that they might be better served opening a spa on the site instead of an ice plant.

Construction on the spa and hotel started in 1913, and were completed by 1914. The hotel was five stories high and done in a beige stucco Italian Villa style. The inside was very ornate with terrazzo floors and marble staircases. Art glass was on display throughout and every modern amenity at the time was in place. The hotel was a near-immediate success.

The pool in the basement of the hotel was the most popular attraction of the hotel. Stories began to circulate that the water had remarkable healing properties. People swarmed to Alton from all over the country to swim in the pool waters. In the local area, people took swimming lessons in the pool and water polo clubs were formed. A supposed doctor by the name of Furlong started to promote and offer hydrotherapy baths which allegedly left those who took them feeling refreshed and healed.

It turns out the Mineral Springs Hotel had a pretty smart marketing department at the time. They began to spread word of the healing properties of the water and then started marketing bottled versions of the water. Starting in 1914, the Mineral Springs Hotel began bottling, selling, and shipping water across the country. In 1914, 350 gallons a week were being consumed. The marketers stressed the healing powers of the water and it began to be billed as being more healing than the water in Hot Springs, Arkansas. Alton, Illinois suddenly found itself on the map and experiencing a major tourist trade. Records from the time indicate that, at one point, the swimming pool attracted over 3,000 people in a single season.

The pool was billed as the "Largest Swimming Pool in Illinois." Parties and receptions were held there. The hotel enjoyed huge success in the early 1900s and the 1920s. Even Hollywood actress Marie Dressler spoke at the hotel, and other celebrities were known to visit and enjoy the pool's healing powers.

Eventually, the Luer family sold the hotel. August Luer sold the property in 1926, but the hotel remained open for many decades after that. In fact, the pool and the hotel remained open well past World War II. The place began to fall on hard times in the 1950s, and the pool was eventually sealed off from public use in 1971.

Like so many buildings with a rich history, it was hard to keep an ornate building down. In 1978, the building reopened as a mall with restaurants and shops. Eventually, it became what it is today, an antiques mall, and the building began to see new life. Granted, it was nothing compared to the crowds the hotel saw when it was supposed to heal guests with magical water, but it still thrives today. It was when the hotel started its life as a mall that stories about restless spirits began to circulate.

While any old hotel could potentially contain the spirits of hundreds of people, the Mineral Springs Hotel reportedly contains the spirits of three people. The first and the most benign of the spirits is reportedly that of an artist who stayed at the hotel in its heyday, but soon found himself unable to pay for his room. Today, if you enter the antique store that stands where the ornately decorated bar once stood, you can see all that remains from that era. There is a mural along one wall, still unfinished, of the city of Alton. According to legend, this mural was painted by the artist as a way of repaying the hotel for his bill.

Supposedly, the young artist died before he could finish the mural. Exactly what he died of it unclear, but apparently he has been unable to leave his work of art. Of course, he is also unable to complete it. According to legend, this man is sometimes seen standing outside the store that was once the bar. He is often seen standing there as though lost, unable to understand where he is. Some report that he looks inebriated. Some even have stated they smell alcohol coming from him if, of course, it is possible for a supposed spirit to smell of alcohol.

The next spirit who supposedly still resides in the old hotel may be a little more frightening, and maybe even potentially harmful. This is the spirit of a man who likes to reside near the pool area. Although these days the pool area is closed off to the public, it is still accessible and there is still a pool there. This man seems to want more than to move things around or scare a few people; legend has it that this spirit is looking for revenge.

The spirit reportedly goes back to the hotels heyday in the 1920s, and during the time when the hotel was holding a lavish black-tie ball. A couple attending the party, held in the pool area, were experiencing some marital problems. The husband was accused by his wife of having an affair. Apparently, his tendencies had come out during this particular party and the husband was spotted by his wife flirting and dancing with several of the young female guests.

His wife evidently reached the breaking point and she charged her husband, having a very loud fight with him. She accused him of flirting and having an affair. Rumor has it that he laughed off her accusations and tried to push her away. This further enraged his wife and she removed one of her shoes. Turning the heel toward her husband's face she smashed him with the shoe.

Her husband staggered, clutching at his face with blood pouring out from the wound. He collided with one of the columns that stands near the pool. Blinded from the blood and the pain, he drifted toward the edge of the pool and then fell in. The party went on around him and by the time anyone realized there was a problem, he'd drowned. Exactly where his wife went or what happened to her is unknown.

The spirit of this man is said to be still lurking near the now-closed pool beneath the antique mall. He is routinely seen standing near the pool dressed in his black tie and tails. Needless to say, he is angry and not a friendly ghost, he scowls and glares at those who see him. Reportedly, he remains there seeking revenge. He is waiting for his wife to show up again, so that this time he can jump her and drown her in the pool. In the meantime, those who report seeing this angry-looking man lurking in the dark basement say they just try to avoid him. No one wants to be a victim of a case of mistaken identity.

The third spirit of the Mineral Springs Hotel is probably the one that is most seen. Much like the "Lavender Lady" from the Lemp Mansion, this ghost has a signature scent, but this one is called the "Jasmine Lady." Also, like some other ghostly activities, this particular spirit seems doomed to relive the gruesome and violent manner of her death over and over again. Some clairvoyants say that these kinds of replay hauntings are not from ghosts who are aware of what is going on. They say that sometimes these events are just so traumatic and violent that the buildings themselves absorb the energy and then are replayed like a videotape over and over again. Although the "Jasmine Lady" apparently performs poltergeist-like activities as well.

In the case of the "Jasmine Lady," she was reportedly a ghost who haunted the hotel when it was still a hotel. Her favorite place to be seen was the staircase located a few steps from what had been the main lobby. The reason she likes to hang out there is where things get gruesome and, once again, infidelity is the main reason for her haunting.

The legend says this woman was a guest at the hotel. Her husband was staying there as well. This time, however, it is the wife who seems to have had a wandering eye. This time, the wife became involved with another man as the couple enjoyed the healing waters reputed to be bubbling in the basement. One day, while here husband was away, she took the man to their room. While in the midst of their act of infidelity, the husband came back and found the two of them in bed—fully involved. As you might expect, the discovery not only ruined his vacation, but made the husband very angry.

This is where the waters of this legend get a little muddy. Exactly what happened next is not fully explained, as is often the case with ghost tales. Supposedly, the argument that ensued ended when the woman ran from the room toward the staircase. Either she tripped as she ran down the stairs or her angered husband caught up with her and pushed her down the stairs. Regardless of why the woman tumbled down the stairs and when she stopped, her neck was broken and she was quite dead. Her husband allegedly walked back to their room where he committed suicide.

Visitors and people who work in the mall have reported seeing this terrible fall down the stairs repeated over and over again. The other common report with this woman is the scent of jasmine near the stairs and other places in the building. Even the owner of the building, a reported ghost skeptic, has said he has smelled the scent of jasmine without explanation. Visitors have also reported finding the powerful scent drifting in the building without a visible or noticeable cause.

Other visitors have correlated a sudden chill or feeling of a presence walking past them with the smell of jasmine. One woman claims that after feeling the chill and smelling the scent, she looked up to see the signs that hang from the walls to mark the stores, swinging back and forth. It was as if something was walking past them hitting them and making them swing. The woman decided that this was enough shopping for one day.

Others who have spent time in the building have experienced the cold chills. They also report the usual unexplained footsteps in empty corridors and laughter and voices in empty rooms. Others report objects moving on their own and, of course, there are the actual apparitions. Given the sheer number of people who spent time in the hotel during its heyday, it's hard to know if those three spirits are the only ones in the hotel. Reports that have been compiled seem to indicate activity much larger than just the three who seem confined to certain areas of the hotel.

The Mineral Springs Hotel is still open as an antiques mall. If you happen to visit Alton, you can find the building and the mall at 301 East Broadway. It's right in the middle of what is known as the Antiques District. You might want to call first to check on the hours, as they can vary from one season to the next. Reportedly, the place still looks enough like a hotel that you almost expect to see guests walking around with luggage. Maybe when you shop, you'll see the "Jasmine Lady" taking her tumble down the stairs or smell her scent. You might see an artist standing outside the store pondering his mural. The pool area is closed off to the public, which may be for the best, as you probably don't want to run into the man in the black tie and tails waiting to seek revenge against his wife.

Conclusions:
Haunted Ground

There are other haunted places in St. Louis. For some reason, the city and surrounding areas are rife with tales of hauntings and ghostly visits. At one time there was a local morning radio show that would broadcast from a supposedly haunted place every Halloween. The entire show would be spend with a visit to the place and would begin broadcasting at midnight on the night of Halloween. They would explore the house with psychics and ghost-hunters. They started out by visiting all of the haunted places generally mentioned in this book, providing memorable broadcasts in the McPike Mansion, among others.

I got to know the two men who hosted this show at one time. As I became acquainted, I knew that some of the things they did during their morning show were faked. They did them for entertainment purposes and for a joke. I asked them about their haunted house broadcasts—how much of that was faked, I wanted to know.

I was told that most of the events described and broadcasted during those shows were real. Yes, they had elaborated on some things beyond what was heard a few times, but I was assured that all of the events described were real and had been witnessed by all members of the show. The ghostly mist with red eyes seen at one place had actually been seen by the show's producer.

When they ran out of the famous places to visit, they began to solicit suggestions from their audience. Perhaps not surprisingly they received numerous responses. It seemed that everyone knew someone who knew of a haunted house. Some of the recordings and EVPs from these places were likely to chill you to the bone.

During the time I lived in St. Louis, I heard several times that it was one of the most haunted cities in the world. After a while, I came to believe that this may, indeed, be the case. As to why this might be, it's hard to say, but there are some theories that might fit as floated by people who claim to be ghost hunters.

There are some who claim that the fact that most of Missouri sits neatly on a bed of limestone may be to blame—most of the city of St. Louis is lined with limestone caves. There have even been tours of the caves given from time to time. One legend says that a cave not far from the Lemp Mansion is haunted by the ghosts of a Native American couple who starved to death inside. Those who have been there claim they hear voices speaking in a strange tongue or hear weeping.

As with so many ghost tales, this one involves love and wronged lovers. This story tells of a Native American couple who got involved, but weren't supposed to. An angry chief chased them down to the caves and then laid siege, and the couple starved to death and died.

The theory espoused by those who claim to hunt ghosts is that limestone and other minerals retain energy, such as that emitted by a human. When especially traumatic things happen, these energies get even more intense and are recorded in the minerals. At times, the energies build up and have to be released, and that's why places on limestone are rife with ghost stories. The ghosts, they imply, are really recorded images or stored energies that mess with the human mind.

Of course, much of St. Louis and parts of Illinois are located over ground considered holy by Native Americans. As mentioned, there was once a city as big as London located in Cahokia, Illinois. In addition to the burial grounds, there was even something called "Woodhenge" located there. Similar to the English Stonehenge, this monument was constructed of wood poles in the ground and in a circle.

Whether or not the Indians were sensing the supposed mystical properties of limestone or perhaps sensed the power of the Mississippi,what is known is that the area around St. Louis has been inhabited for a very long time. In that time, a lot of people died and a lot of people were buried. If you subscribe to the idea of burial grounds still holding spirits, then maybe that could explain why spirits still roam.

Old buildings with ancient architecture still dot much of the St. Louis area and the areas surrounding it. While other cities seem to have tried very hard to tear down the older buildings to make way for newer ones, the St. Louis area seems to have weathered better than others. Perhaps some spirits simply like to stay in these old buildings as they change to commercial and then residential properties.

Like many old cities, St. Louis is also dotted with old cemeteries. Walking through them is like walking through history. In some cases, the tombstones themselves are terrifying to look at. Some have pictures of the deceased on the stones—and the pictures are old and they stare back at you. In each case, the cemeteries have tales of spirits and hauntings.

Of course, the power of suggestion is also very prominent. Walking through the Lemp Mansion, for example, is creepy from the get-go. The place is old and dark and dusty despite all attempts to keep it clean. The ceilings are high despite the fact the Lemps themselves were notoriously short. Since the place itself is famous for being haunted, when you walk up the steps toward the white front and see all of the wrought iron and ancient brickwork, you can't help but feel just a little creeped out.

The management of the place has also placed pictures around to add to the creepiness. In the room where I stayed, there was one picture so creepy that my roommate and myself had to take it down and face it toward the wall. The eyes seemed to follow you and were so lifelike it was almost as if the peasant girl in the likeness would step down off the wall and walk towards you.

You walk up creaky stairs covered with thick dark carpet. Portraits line the walls. Stained glass looks down from the walls in the bar area. The place even smells old and maybe haunted.

Tales from the McPike Mansion are wide and varied and come in styles from the terrifying to the ridiculous. It's a large ancient house with broken windows and a sagging floor that seems to *look* haunted. Since it looks haunted, people have just assumed that it is. In the neighborhood where you grew up, there was probably an old house or building that was always empty and got the reputation for being haunted.

The same could be said for the old McDowell Medical College which sat empty and broken and dark in its neighborhood for many years before it was finally torn down. With all of the broken windows and just the right kind of wind, it might have created the kind of moaning reported to have been heard in the surrounding neighborhood.

No one can say for sure what does or does not lurk in the old buildings and cemeteries and limestone caves that make up St. Louis. If you believe in ghosts, then perhaps you see ghosts. On the other hand, my night in the Lemp Mansion made me see and hear things that I still cannot entirely explain.

Whatever the reason, St. Louis is a haunted city. It's a modern city, but it has a long past. It seems that, to some, the past still likes to peek through into today. What can be known is that the legends and stories are likely to continue and likely to grow as the years go by.

The following was prepared by Scott Lefebvre, published author and staff writer for Scars Magazine.

Email Scott at: Scott_Lefebvre@hotmail.com.

Guide for Urban Exploration

If you're anything like me, creepy looking abandoned buildings have an almost irresistible attraction as destinations for adventurous excursions.

Attractive destinations include any abandoned buildings, usually the older the better, and especially asylums and churches, ex-military bases, and anything else interesting and off limits.

We all know that trespassing is illegal, but if you're as irresistibly attracted to these destinations as I am, there are a few things that you may want to keep in mind.

Many urban explorers bring back small souvenirs from their excursions. I still have two coffee mugs from the Ladd Center, which are precious to me. But I ask that if you do decide to visit someplace with the purpose of exploring it, that you avoid the urge to destroy or vandalize anything while you're there. Everyone loves the sound of breaking glass, and it's sometimes gratifying to leave your mark for future explorers to discover, but please think about preserving the site for other explorers. Vandalism only serves to increase security surveillance or make the site more likely to face destruction as a safety hazard and a popular destination for unwanted visitors. It's perfectly acceptable to take as many pictures as you desire, but the best souvenir will be your memory of the experience.

Things that you might want to remember to bring along with you.

If your planned destination is a building, day or night, you'll want to bring a flashlight. If you enter an abandoned building, there will most likely be rooms that do not have direct access to the outside and will be dark without artificial light. It's also important to always be able to see where you're planning on going. The most common injuries for urban explorers are tripping over something underfoot because they weren't watching where they were going or hitting their head or getting cut by something hanging down from overhead.

My favorite flashlight is the Mag-Lite mini. It's more expensive than the one-use flashlights that you can buy at the register or get for free as a promotional item with a pack of batteries but it's infinitely more reliable and durable. It will survive a few accidental drops onto concrete floors, and the bulbs are cheap and replaceable. The light it throws is bright and clear and adjustable, and it's relatively cheap so it won't be a big deal if you drop it someplace that you can't easily retrieve it. It runs on double A's and gets pretty good battery life, but make sure you bring spare batteries. You don't want to be trapped in an unfamiliar, potentially dangerous environment with a handful of dead flashlight.

A camera with a good flash is also highly recommended. Digital cameras are lighter and often cheaper than film cameras and can take a lot of pictures without requiring the user to play around with loading in a new roll of film in a dusty, musty environment. Plus if you have to run you don't want a bulky film camera with a flash attachment bumping around. Some of the most common sad stories about urban exploration are about broken or lost film cameras. Don't be one of those people.

Tying back long hair and wearing a baseball hat is recommended. You don't want your hair to accidentally get snagged on something and get pulled out. If you're going to hit your head on something it's better to get your hat knocked off than to get a rusty cut. Wear sensible shoes. Sneakers with thick, skid-proof soles, or even better, work boots. The floors of abandoned buildings are often cluttered with debris and filth and sometimes damp or flooded. Also keep in mind that you may have to run and hide from security or police, so please be smart and tie your shoes. But only run if you're outside. Even a familiar spot might have changed since the last time you were there. Running in an unfamiliar environment is easily the best way to accidentally hurt yourself seriously while urban exploring.

You may want to bring light work gloves. Not so much to avoid leaving fingerprints, but more because abandoned buildings can be dirty places. There are rusty ladders and stairwell handrails and the walls are usually moldy. Anywhere you put your hands you can pick up dirt and you don't want that kind of dirt in your eyes or mouth. It's better to get your glove snagged on something sharp instead of cutting your hand open.

And speaking of mold and dust, if you're predisposed to allergies, you may want to invest in a good dust mask. In some old buildings there's lead paint dust and asbestos. I'm not too worried about breathing in a little toxic dust, but some of you may not be so careless.

Finally, as I've stated earlier, we all know that trespassing is illegal. If you're uncomfortable with possible legal involvement, there are many excellent places of supernatural interest that are perfectly legal to visit and explore.

It's important to keep in mind that even going onto property that is not public can be considered trespassing. If you enter into an abandoned building that can be considered illegal entry and trespassing. And if you had to do anything to a window or door to get into a building it becomes breaking and entering.

If you do get caught, which sometimes does happen, remain calm. Don't make an awkward situation worse. Treat whoever apprehends you with due respect and politeness. Sometimes you can pretend that you didn't know that it was illegal to trespass at the site. If that doesn't work, calmly and politely explain that you wanted to visit the location, but your intention was to explore and take pictures, while showing them your camera, not to break things and put up graffiti, and that while you were exploring you were careful not to accidentally damage anything and you are quite sorry and do not plan on returning. You might get your camera taken away, but that beats having to spend a day at court dressed in your really nice clothes and maybe having to do twenty hours of community service or something lame like that.

On a final note, I implore you to not bring any weapons along with you while urban exploring. Having a small pocketknife or pocket multi-tool like a Swiss Army knife or a Leatherman can be convenient and handy, especially if your hair or clothes get snagged and you have to cut yourself loose. But it's completely unnecessary to bring a big hunting knife, or even worse, a handgun, along for the trip. If you're looking for ghosts, a weapon won't do you any good against them. Having a weapon just makes it that much more likely that someone will accidentally get hurt, and getting caught while urban exploring just gets more complicated if you're running around with a samurai sword.

Please be smart, be safe, and send me a set of your awesome pictures.

Or even better, take me a long on your next trip.

* The following section is provided by the Chester County Paranormal Research Society in Pennsylvania and appears in training materials for new investigators.

Please visit www.ChesterCountyprs.com for more information.

Glossary and Equipment List

Air Probe Thermometer

A thermometer with an external probe that is capable of taking instant measurements of the air temperature.

Anomalous field

A field that can not be explained or ruled out by various possibilities, that can be a representation of spirit or paranormal energy present.

Apparition

A transparent form of a human or animal, a spirit.

Artificial field

A field that is caused by electrical outlets, appliances, etc.

Aural Enhancer

A listening device that enhances or amplifies audio signals. i.e., Orbitor Bionic Ear.

Automatic writing

The act of a spirit guiding a human agent in writing a message that is brought through by the spirit.

Base readings
The readings taken at the start of an investigation and are used as a means of comparing other readings taken later during the course of the investigation.

Demonic Haunting
A haunting that is caused by an inhuman or subhuman energy or spirit.

Dowsing Rods
A pair of L-shaped rods or a single Y-shaped rod, used to detect the presence of what the person using them is trying to find.

Electro-static generator
A device that electrically charges the air often used in paranormal investigations/research as a means to contribute to the materialization of paranormal or spiritual energy.

ELF
Extremely Low Frequency.

ELF Meter/EMF Meter
A device that measures electric and magnetic fields.

EMF
Electro Magnetic Field.

EVP
Electronic Voice Phenomena.

False positive
Something that is being interpreted as paranormal within a picture or video and is, in fact, a natural occurrence or defect of the equipment used.

Gamera

A 35mm film camera connected with a motion detector that is housed in a weather proof container and takes a picture when movement is detected. Made by Silver Creek Industries.

Geiger Counter

A device that measures gamma and x-ray radiation.

Infra Red

An invisible band of radiation at the lower end of the visible light spectrum. With wavelengths from 750 nm to 1 mm, infrared starts at the end of the microwave spectrum and ends at the beginning of visible light. Infrared transmission typically requires an unobstructed line of sight between transmitter and receiver. Widely used in most audio and video remote controls, infrared transmission is also used for wireless connections between computer devices and a variety of detectors.

Intelligent haunting

A haunting of a spirit or other entity that has the ability to interact with the living and do things that can make its presence known.

Milli-gauss

Unit of measurement, measures in 1000th of a gauss and is named for the famous German mathematician, Karl Gauss.

Orbs

Anomalous spherical shapes that appear on video and still photography.

Pendulum

A pointed item that is hung on the end of a string or chain and is used as a means of contacting spirits. An individual will hold the item and let it hang from the finger tips. The individual will ask questions aloud and the pendulum answers by moving.

Poltergeist haunting

A haunting that has two sides, but same kinds of activity in common. Violent outbursts of activity with doors and windows slamming shut, items being thrown across a room and things being knocked off of surfaces. Poltergeist hauntings are usually focused around a specific individual who resides or works at the location of the activity reported, and, in some cases, when the person is not present at the location, activity does not occur. A poltergeist haunting may be the cause of a human agent or spirit/energy that may be present at the location.

Portal

An opening in the realm of the paranormal that is a gateway between one dimension and the next. A passageway for spirits to come and go through. See also Vortex.

Residual haunting

A haunting that is an imprint of an event or person that plays itself out like a loop until the energy that causes it has burned itself out.

Scrying

The act of eliciting information with the use of a pendulum from spirits.

Table Tipping

A form of spirit communication, the act of a table being used as a form of contact. Individuals will sit around a table and lightly place there fingertips on the edge of the table and elicit contact with a spirit. The Spirit will respond by "tipping" or moving the table.

Talking Boards

A board used as a means of communicating with a spirit. Also known as a Quija Board.

Vortex

A place or situation regarded as drawing into its center all that surrounds it.

White Noise

A random noise signal that has the same sound energy level at all frequencies.

Equipment List

In this section, the Chester County Paranormal Research Society looks at the application and benefits of equipment used on investigations with greater detail. The equipment used for an investigation plays a vital role in the ability to collect objective evidence and helps to determine what *is* and *is not* paranormal activity. But a key point to be made here is: the investigator is the most important tool on any investigation. With that said, let us now take a look at the main pieces of equipment used during an investigation...

The Geiger Counter

The Geiger counter is device that measures radiation. A "Geiger counter" usually contains a metal tube with a thin metal wire along its middle. The space in between them is sealed off and filled with a suitable gas and with the wire at about +1000 volts relative to the tube.

An ion or electron penetrating the tube (or an electron knocked out of the wall by X-rays or gamma rays) tears electrons off atoms in the gas. Because of the high positive voltage of the central wire, those electrons are then attracted to it. They gain energy that collide with atoms and release more electrons, until the process snowballs into an "avalanche", producing an easily detectable pulse of current. With a suitable filling gas, the flow of electricity stops by itself, or else the electrical circuitry can help stop it.

The instrument was called a "counter" because every particle passing it produced an identical pulse, allowing particles to be counted, usually electronically. But it did not tell anything about their identity or energy, except that they must have sufficient energy to penetrate the walls of the counter.

The Geiger counter is used in paranormal research to measure the background radiation at a location. The working theory in this field is that paranormal activity can effect the background radiation. In some cases, it will increase the radiation levels and in other cases it will decrease the levels.

Digital and 35mm Film Cameras

The camera is an imperative piece of equipment that enabled us to gather objective evidence during a case. Some of the best evidence presented from cases of paranormal activity over the years has been because of photographs taken. If you own your own digital camera or 35mm film camera, you need to be fully aware of what the cameras abilities and limitations are. Digital cameras have been at the center of great debate in the field of paranormal research over the years.

The earlier incarnations of digital cameras were full of inherent problems and notorious for creating "false positive" pictures. A "false positive" picture is a picture that has anomalous elements within the picture that are the result of a camera defect or other natural occurrence. There are many pictures scattered about the internet that claim to be of true paranormal activity, but in fact they are "false positives." Orbs, defined as anomalous paranormal energy that can show up as balls of light or streaks in still photography or video, are the most controversial pictures of paranormal energy in the field. There are so many theories (good and bad) about the origin of orbs and what they are. Every picture in the CCPRS collection that has an orb—or orbs—are not presented in a way that state that they are absolutely paranormal of nature. I have yet to capture an orb photo that made me feel certain that in fact it is of a paranormal nature.

If you use your own camera, understand that your camera is vital. I encourage all members who own their own cameras to do research on the make and model of the camera and see what other consumers are saying about them. Does the manufacturer give any info regarding possible defects or design flaws with that particular model? Understanding your camera will help to rule out the possibility of interpreting a "false positive" for an authentic picture of paranormal activity.

Video Cameras

The video camera is also a fundamental tool in the investigation as another way for collecting objective evidence that can support the proof of paranormal activity. The video camera can be used in various ways during the investigation. It can be set on a tripod and left in a location where paranormal activity has been reported. It can also be used as a hand-held camera and the investigator will take it with them during their walk through investigation as a means of documenting to hopefully capture anomalous activity on tape. Infra-Red technology has become a feature on most consumer level video cameras and depending on the manufacturer can be called "night shot" or "night alive." What this technology does is allow us to use the camera in zero light. Most cameras with this feature will add a green tint or haze to the camera when it is being used in this mode. A video camera with this ability holds great appeal to the paranormal investigator.

EMF/ELF Meters

EMF=Electro Magnetic Frequency   ELF=Extremely Low Frequency

What is an EMF/ELF meter? Good question. The EMF/ELF meter is a meter that measures Electric and Magnetic fields in an AC or DC current field. It measures in a unit of measurement called "milli-gauss," named for the famous German mathematician, Karl Gauss. Most meters will measure in a range of 1-5 or 1-10 milli-gauss. The reason that EMF meters are used in paranormal research is because of the theory that a spirit or paranormal energy can add to the energy field when it is materializing or is present in a location. The theory says that, typically, an energy that measures between 3-7 milli-gauss may be of a paranormal origin. This doesn't mean that an artificial field can't also measure within this range. That is why we take base readings and make maps notating where artificial fields occur. The artificial fields are a direct result of electricity, i.e. wiring, appliances, light switches, electrical outlets, circuit breakers, high voltage power lines, sub-stations, etc.

The Earth emits a naturally occurring magnetic field all around us and has an effect on paranormal activity. Geo-magnetic storm activity can also have a great influence on paranormal activity. For more information on this kind of phenomena visit: www.noaa.sec. com.

There are many different types of EMF meters; and each one, although it measures with the same unit of measurement, may react differently. An EMF meter can range from anywhere to $12.00 to $1,000.00 or more depending on the quality and features that it has. Most meters are measuring the AC (alternating current, the type of fields created by man-made electricity) fields and some can measure DC (direct current-naturally occurring fields, batteries also fall into the category of DC) fields. The benefit of having a meter that can measure DC fields is that they will automatically filter out the artificial fields created by AC fields and can pick up more naturally occurring electro magnetic fields. Some of the higher-tech EMF meters are so sensitive that they can pick up the fields generated by living beings. The EMF meter was originally designed to measure the earth's magnetic fields and also to measure the fields created by electrical an artificial means.

There have been various studies over the years about the long term effects of individuals living in or near high fields. There has been much controversy as to whether or not long term exposure to high fields can lead to cancer. It has been proven though that no matter what, long term exposure to high fields can be harmful to your health. The ability to locate these high fields within a private residence or business is vital to the investigation. We may offer suggestions to the client as to possible solutions for dealing with high fields. The wiring in a home or business can greatly affect the possibility of high fields. If the wiring is old and/or not shielded correctly, it can emit high fields that may affect the ability to correctly notate any anomalous fields that may be present.

Audio Recording Equipment

Audio recording equipment is used for conducting EVP (Electronic Voice Phenomena) research and experiments. What is an EVP? An EVP is a phenomenon where paranormal voices or sounds can be captured with audio recording devices. The theory is that the activity will imprint directly onto the device or tape, but has not been proven to be an absolute fact. The use of an external microphone is essential when conducting EVP experiments with analog recording equipment. The internal microphone on an analog tape recorder can pick up the background noise of the working parts within the tape recorder and can taint the evidence as a whole. Most digital recorders are quiet enough to use the internal microphone, but as a general rule of thumb, we do not use them. An external microphone will be used always. Another theory about EVP research is that an authentic EVP will happen within the range 250-400hz. This is a lower frequency range and isn't easily heard by the human ear, and the human voice does not emit in this range. EVP is rarely heard at the moment it happens—it is usually revealed during the playback and analysis portion of the investigation.

Thermometers

The use of a thermometer in an investigation goes without saying. This is how we monitor the temperature changes during the course of an investigation. CCPRS is currently using Digital thermometers with remote sensors as a way to set up a perimeter and to notate any changes in a stationary location of an investigation. The Air-probe thermometer can take "real time" readings that are instantly accurate. This is the more appropriate thermometer for measuring air temperature and "cold spots" that may be caused by the presence of paranormal phenomena. The IR Non-contact thermometer is the most misused thermometer in the field of paranormal research. CCPRS does not own or use IR Non-contact thermometers for this reason. The IR (infra-red) Non-contact thermometer is meant for measuring surface temperatures from a remote location. It shoots an infrared beam out to an object and bounces to the unit and gives the temperature reading. I have seen, first hand, investigators using this thermometer as a way to measure air temperature. NO, this is not correct! Enough said. In an email conversation that I have had with Grant Wilson from TAPS, he has said that, "Any change in temperature that can't be measured with your hand is not worth notating…"